*IN MEMORY OF MY COUSIN
STU ARNOLD
1951–1996*

Contents

S T O R Y
S T A R T E R S

Introduction

Story Starters is for writers what Impromptu Theater is for actors.

When Mike Nichols and Elaine May were struggling students at the University of Chicago, they hung out at a local bar where the regulars would buy the beer in return for comedy routines invented on the spot. Nichols and May became rich and famous beginning with those stories started from suggestions by the patrons. By the time they left Chicago, they had polished a cache of material they were to use for years. I wrote *Story Starters* because I'm convinced the process works for writers.

Evidence abounds. This book is crammed with anecdotes about writers who found ideas for stories from sources other than their own imaginations. Some are well known. Others, like you, hope to be.

William Faulkner saw a little girl with muddy drawers climbing a tree. The image, recorded in his notebook, became the stimulus for his classic, *The Sound and the Fury.*

Paul Byerly, a writer in my New School class, went to a fancy dinner party. The affluent host said when he was young, his father had promised to buy him a bike, but reneged, so he stole one. Paul never saw the man again, but he put the remark in his notebook. Eventually, he wrote a novel, *How to Steal a Bicycle.* Paul's protagonist stole fifty-two.

1

Several writers have found a tale to be told in a wave, not the wet kind, but in the flutter of a hand. Peter Sis was still a foreigner to our culture, and lonely, when he thought a friendly New Yorker was waving to him, but she was hailing a cab. He wrote it down and now kids see it happen in *Waving*. I've always wanted to pull that chap out of Stevie Smith's poem and wrap him up in a story. You know, the one who said, "I was much too far out all my life/ And not waving but drowning."

Eudora Welty lived as uneventful a life as Emily Brontë, but look at the stories they wrote. Welty took ideas from photographs she shot while working as a newspaper society editor. Barbara Lucas, a writer in my workshop, swears she saw a vision of the entire plot for her complex novel appear from a picture postcard, the reproduction of an eighteenth-century painting.

Norma Klein saw a newspaper story that went into her notebook, but wouldn't stay put. A teenage couple in South Carolina traded their baby for a red Camaro, the article said. The plot for Norma's novel, *The Swap,* is woven around the used-car salesman and the baby with the big ears.

Each summer I rent a big house next door to mine on Bailey Island in Maine and invite ten writers to come for a workshop. They find stories in the thunderous waves rising one above the other into the air, the cry of the gulls with the old, crabby faces.

Don't be discouraged if you want to write but have not found your material. Stay with me. You will. Not all good writers have a stash of stories waiting to be told. Legend has it, on the Oakland waterfront, around the turn of the last century, Jack London—to pay for his supper—sold plot proposals to other writers. You won't have to, but some novelists have even gone to extremes searching for tales. Hemingway almost got himself killed by bulls and bullets to have experiences to write about, and Fitzgerald ruined his liver looking for material at parties for the rich.

Granted, many soldiers came back from Vietnam determined to update *Heart of Darkness,* and many young people returned from the bright lights of the big-city streets having found their muse in clubs and drugs. But just because someone wants to write, she doesn't have to have faced the grim reaper, ruined her nose with coke, or had a long session with a Scotch bottle.

Story Starters contains not only a myriad of ideas for characters, settings, and themes to be developed into narratives, but a process for learning how to think like a writer and create them yourself. Think of yourself as a Rolls Royce with a dead battery, the exercises as a jumper cable.

Picture this: A woman sits on the floor of her flat, surrounded by dusty, unopened, moving cartons packed seventeen months ago. Moonbeams, the only light, spill in the window. Think like a writer:

How old is she? What is she wearing? Is her expression sad, smug, scared, sneering? Where is this apartment? What sounds does she hear? Do they come from outside or within her head? What time is it? What year? What is her name? Why is she there? What is packed in the boxes? Why doesn't she open them? What does it mean? Tell your typewriter about her. Then just try to forget her. She will stick with you until you tell her story. Believe it.

Before we go any further, however, I must warn you. Thinking like a writer will change your life. You think your Aunt Mable was a nag? Wait until you find a character who insists you tell his story. A glorious Indian summer day peaks flirtatiously through the sliding glass door—maybe the last of the season—you start to put on your walking shoes, but your protagonist begins: "You're going out and leaving me in the middle of chapter seven with the most important decision of my life yet to be made? You'll lose the momentum, wear yourself out, slow down the pacing. . . ." So you untie the laces, turn on the computer, and when you look up again, the man in the moon winks at you.

Writing can be as addictive as computer games. Your plan might be to pick just one idea, write one short story some rainy Sunday afternoon—just to see if you can do it—just for the fun of it, but writing is like eating only one cashew from a full bowl. Getting hooked on writing stories is not a bad habit, but I strongly suggest you not take your laptop on your honeymoon.

You won't have to quite your day job. Writers in my workshops and New School classes continue to design

costumes for Broadway shows, work in the library, put
on their hard hats, drive cabs, deliver sailboats, report
the news, raise kids, teach school, fact check for magazines. But as we go to press, two successful lawyers *have*
given notice. It will be okay. They both write better than
John Grisham.

Here is the way thinking like a writer works. All you
need is a sturdy notebook and all your senses function-
ing. I had a lunch date with Taddy, a friend from Washington, D.C., whom I had not seen for months. I was in
the shower when the phone rang. Let the machine pick
it up? Better not. My sister had problems to solve, a
friend's mother had had a massive stroke, an intriguing
gentleman had asked for my card at the last book
discussion. . . . I grabbed a robe. It was Stephen, my
editor, the one whose voice sounds cheerful, even when
he is saying you spell funny, put commas in the darndest
places, and no, he wishes he could but absolutely cannot
get you a bigger advance.

"How would you like to do a book called *Story Starters?*"
Stephen asked. I had already written *So You Want to Write
a Novel,* but the theory had evolved from my New School
classes. All I had to do was put it in the computer. My
father, dead for too many years, had insisted upon dictat-
ing *Writing Your Life: Putting Your Past on Paper.* Making
him stop talking was the biggest problem.

"Hmmm . . . Let me get back to you, Stephen."

Story starters? A woman is in the shower . . . the phone
rings . . . she snatches a robe . . . a blue terry-cloth robe
with a frayed collar . . . or is it lilac, the slick polyester
fabric dotted with nubs from too many washings . . . or
sleek silk, black with red piping and a monogram? . . . Her
wet skin begins to feels prickly—prickly is a delicious word.
The voice on the phone says . . ."

Fortunately, Taddy is a good sport. I was late. My skin
itched. I wrote notes on my napkin . . . and hers. I asked
to borrow her name—sometimes just a name will launch a
story. We probably wouldn't have gone whaling, but I am
sure I could have found a story for a man named Quee-
queg. Taddy's name has definite possibilities.

Taddy and I ate at P. J. Clarke's, an East Side literary

watering hole that smells like fried onions. Okay, so most New Yorkers with ink-stained fingers have already set at least one scene in P.J.'s—many with the ghost of James Baldwin standing at the bar—but usually the saloon serves only as a backdrop. There's more here. This place is a tough character. After so many knockouts, City Hall no longer even asks for a rematch. The squatty little pub holds its ground between towering office buildings like a bully with his hands on his hips daring an interloper to invade his territory with a wrecking ball.

After lunch Taddy, a Texan raised to know how to do the dip floor curtsy, needed a new watchband. Cartier has many mirrors, two floors, and an elevator with a padded seat. No one raises their voice at Cartier, even if the service is slow and the chauffeur is getting a parking ticket for loitering on Fifth Avenue.

The willowy woman serving Taddy looked like Iman. An NBA center would have to stand on tiptoes to kiss her, even if she weren't wearing "if you've got it flaunt it" five-inch heels. Her legs were four times as long as her skirt. We had to wait while the lady with legs like stilts put the band on Taddy's watch.

Readers—and editors—like story titles that deliver what they promise, and they are easier to write. It's like having a map. "I Don't Have a Cartier Watch, But I Have Friends Who Do" comes with a built-in voice and tone. I wrote the possible title on the back of a Cartier catalogue. When you begin to think like a writer, never leave home without your notebook. The napkins from PJ's were soggy and the catalogue wouldn't fit in my bag.

Later that afternoon, when I called Stephen to tell him I would do the book, I thought he would be impressed with the story starters I had found on my lunch date. After a while, he said—cheerfully—"Sure . . . great . . . that's a good one . . . terrific . . . put them in the book." Okay, so I will tell you.

If you stay alert, you will find characters searching for an author, plots vying for your attention, no matter where you live, where you kick up your heels, or who signs your paycheck. Every high-rise building has a doorman who could tell tales the residents would blush to read. Consider him as a possible narrator.

I created Faith, a cynical—see all, know all—grumpy assistant to the chairman of a large corporation. There is probably a model for her in your office. Mine was to have a walk-on role, but then I discovered Faith had hemorrhoids that made her cranky, a chronic itch to have the CEO's wife whacked, and a powerhouse mother who promised to live forever. She makes me laugh out loud. I can't let her go.

The evening after agreeing to do the book, a friend and I had tickets for the Jazz Festival at Lincoln Center. I love jazz and tried so hard to listen, but more stories than notes were swirling around that auditorium.

The flumpeter sat apart and still, on a high stool next to the conductor, who paid him deference, as did the other, younger toe-tapping, finger-snapping, head-bopping music makers. An ugly wizened face as ancient as a cathedral gargoyle rose majestically from the flumpeter's baby blue jacket. When he blew his "Walkin' Shoes" solo, not a foot shuffled in the audience, no programs fluttered, no whispers were uttered. He tipped his head once to the roaring applause he had grown accustomed to a long time ago. When it stopped, the conductor raised his baton and nodded his head to the old man, who got off his stool and walked calmly offstage. Lowering his stick, laughing nervously, the leader said, "Do you suppose he's coming back?" He did—after a while. Nonchalantly, he flipped a note onto the conductor's music stand, picked up his horn, and waited for the beat. Trying not to seem interested in the message, the leader scooted it off his score and struck up "Sweet & Lovely."

The horn player must have had a young man's lip, but an old man's kidneys. He probably had to go to the bathroom, but I'll leave the details to you. The patriarchal flumpeter wore his confidence, but I would love to know what the note said, who sent it, what connection existed among the sender, the messenger, and the conductor. When you write it, make it enticing.

Everyone has a story, if someone would only tell it. Any member of the Lincoln Center Jazz Orchestra could have been a protagonist, especially the short, stocky guy patting, stroking, plucking, tickling his red-hot mamma for all to see. That big fat bass had that man grooving and sweat-

ing rivers. The cool guitar player next to him wore a wise-
acre grin and funny-colored socks. He was young, but that
cool cat already had a history. I would like to spend some
time with him in my computer, but I'm working on something else. He's yours if you want him.

If luck is a lady, long before you work your way through
the ideas on the following pages, you will have a notebook
thicker than this book. My mission is to offer suggestions
until you train your eyes, ears, nose to find stories tucked
in your jewelry box, photo album, morning paper, dear
john letters. You will meet characters on the bus, at the
yacht club, at a PTA meeting, a ball game, your high school
reunion. That's a promise.

Jim, an English major, graduated from college determined to write a book. He just didn't yet know what it
was to be about. Fate takes circuitous routes. As a construction worker, he joined the iron workers' union, became a loyal member. He got married, had a child, but
his goal to write a novel was only turned on low. When
a scandal in the membership began to simmer and finally
boiled over, he turned up in my New School class. He
had his story—a whodunit mystery, he thought. But Jim
is too thoughtful to be constrained by the genre's for-
mula. He probes his character's motivation, fleshes out
his minor characters, and is building toward an Aristote-
lian conclusion. He blushes, but I call him Hamlet in a
hard hat.

Linda, a lawyer, tried a case she could not forget. Her
trial, like Jim's scandal, worked like the starter one needs
for sourdough bread. Linda comes to class somedays with
a skeptical look on her face. "You won't believe whom my
character has fallen for," she says. "A detective? I still can't
believe she's doing this."

Until you find that story you can't not tell, get in shape
with the practice exercises to follow. My mantra is: *You
learn to write by writing.* I have scores of students who
prove the point. Writers, who have to keep more than one
idea activated, are allowed two chants. My second is: *Write
from experience not about it.*

This is the only book I have ever written in which I hope
you don't have to read all of it. If the gods responsible for
writers are working with you, perhaps an idea for your

story will jump out at you right away. However, technical tips are tucked into each chapter. Check the table of contents for suggestions on techniques to add finesse to your fiction.

CHAPTER 1

What If

With my publisher's blessing, I am pleased to offer a life-time gift certificate to all readers of *Story Starters*. The boon, a staple in every author's repertoire, has a touch of magic and has been known to help many a blocked writer to wiggle out of a jam. The present is a phrase: "What if." Don't lose it!

What if you have always wanted to write fiction, teachers have given you good marks, friends tie a blue ribbon around your letters, even your grumpy boss praises your reports, but you look for a subject only to decide your life has the sparkle of a dreary day in March? Change the script. The college prof who told you literature mirrored reality only meant your work had to be credible. Without an imaginative touch up, most of our days would play like movies in very, very slow motion. Someone wise, whose name I've lost, said, "There is no such thing as life. We make up ourselves and others. There are only stories.

Storytellers can make reality what they want it to be. Others must lie."

If there hasn't been a message on your answering machine for five and a half days, you did not get a raise but Peter did, and even your cat won't cuddle, don't write about that. If you prefer action, dream of romance, thrive on mystery, or long for an intellectual challenge, play "what if." What if things had turned out differently? Writers can make things whatever they want them to be.

Here how it works:

Last winter, I was on a long bus trip from Auckland to the Bay of Islands in New Zealand. After a couple of hours, rolling along in the middle of nowhere, the driver announced we would stop for a twenty-minute refreshment break, but there would be several coaches in the lot, so he warned us to be sure to listen for his call.

A scruffy kid with freckles on his nose and no laces in his boots and I did not hear the driver announcing it was time to reboard. He bounced on down the road with our luggage. After a moment of turmoil, I found the boy a ride with a family going in his direction, and another bus driver agreed to detour off his route to pick me up. By midafternoon, I was checked into a charming resort. I had my bags. All was well.

Except . . . I couldn't stop thinking about the boy on the bus. He could have used a pair of shoelaces and a good scrub . . . maybe a friend. . . .

"What if" the woman and the boy had *not* arrived at their destinations? What if, on a whim, they had set out on an adventure? I had talked to the lad only long enough to learn he was sixteen, through with school, and was on his way to visit his mum. Why only "visit" his mum? Why had he quit school? I could not find a switch to turn off the story. Everywhere I went I saw them—the woman and the boy who seemed to want to become my characters. I heard them talking, telling each other their back stories. By the time I had returned to the States, I knew why they did it, where they went, and how their odyssey ended. I put aside what I had been working on before the trip.

The Kiwi boy tells me his name is Trevor Jones, if you can believe it. His friend calls herself Cassie Prince, but that name doesn't match the one on her driver's license issued in Chicago, Illinois. She wears her hair in a long, smooth black braid, just the way I always wanted my curly hair to look. Cassie chose *Mad Money* as a title for their adventure story. They think I'm slow, and I admit I can't type as fast as they talk, but we should finish a draft before Christmas.

Robert Cormier taught me how to play "what if." Before the success of *The Chocolate War* allowed him to write full time, he had been a newspaper reporter raising a large family and writing fiction when he could steal the time. Then one night his fifteen-year-old son said it was time for the kids to sell candy to raise money for the school, but he didn't see how he could spend the time when he was already having trouble keeping up his grades and playing sports. He asked and received Cormier's permission to talk to the priest about being excused from the chocolate sale. The next morning, Cormier dropped his son off at the school but didn't drive away. He watched the boy walk up a long flight of marble steps and thought, "What if. . . ." What if there were an evil priest waiting up there? His son's priest didn't make him sell the candy, but at the top of those stairs Cormier's character, Jerry, meets Brother Leon and a school bully named Archie. All hell breaks loose.

Now you try it. What if there were a message on your answering machine such as:

STORY STARTERS

☞   You can have the promotion, but you will have to relocate to L.A.

☞   Your Uncle Charlie died. His lawyer would like for you to be in his office Wednesday at ten A.M. for the reading of the will.

☞   Dumping you on graduation day was the worst mistake of my life. Shelia and I didn't work out. I'll be at the Colony at eight. I asked the chef to prepare a lemon soufflé and to put white tulips on the table. I hope you still like them, but mainly I hope you will show up.

☞   Some maniac at the Lincoln Elementary School Cafeteria laced the tomato soup with poison this morning.

☞ This is the manager at the Hilltop Country Club. Congratulations, we have done a recount and your membership has been approved.

☞ Hey, Mom, it's me. Sorry to hang this on you, but I've been expelled.

☞ Pal, I hope you won't be upset or anything . . . but, ole buddy, I really need a favor. See, my secretary and I've got this thing going, and if I could just borrow your pad for a few nooners, Thelma would never find out. And don't forget you owe me one, sport.

☞ Sorry to have to deliver such bad news on the phone, but I thought you would want to know as soon as possible. Your whole department is being phased out. Downsizing, you know.

☞ This is State Patrolman Raymond Tucker. There has been an accident.

☞ I'm downstairs in the lobby and that ole fart of a guard won't let me come up with my cart, but I gotta see you right away. I've been living on the street for months now, and think how your poor mother—God rest her soul—would feel if she knew you turned down a first cousin.

☞ Our class reunion has been scheduled for August eighth. We'll just be devastated if you can't make it.

The man with the white tulips waiting for your character at the Colony tickled my imagination, but you can pick your favorite. The process works the same. (The techniques for developing your story will be dealt with in more depth in proceeding chapters.)

ESTABLISHING THE WHERE AND WHEN

To avoid confusion that leads to disinterest, you must let your reader know immediately where and when the story is taking place. You can go back in time or leap to the future, but remember to take your reader with you. Let's say, when your character receives the message from her former beau she is living on a houseboat in Portland,

Maine, ten years after graduating from Boston University in 1986. If the wind were whipping against the windows and the waves slapping the deck, she would be in a more vulnerable mood than if a summer sun were adding sparkle to a gentle surf. It's your call.

Now put a time frame around the actual action of your story. How much time passes after she hears the message until the conclusion? Most narratives require flashbacks, but this one could take place in one day if the problem only focuses on "will she or won't she." But a novel exists in every short story. You could begin on graduation day and the message could be the last page of a four-hundred-and-fifty-page saga.

When you jump around in time and place, tell the reader: Ten years ago in Boston, I had wanted to strangle him. . . . Thirty minutes after hearing the message, I was in a water taxi. . . . When I was a romantic six-year-old growing up in Montreal, I thought . . .

DEVELOPING YOUR CHARACTER

Do the easy part first: What is her name; how old is she; what does she see when she looks in the mirror; what do you? Are her teeth straight? Where is her family; are they supportive; does she like them; how many siblings does she have; is she the firstborn, baby, only daughter, or . . . ? Where does she work? How does she vote? Is she religious? Is she tidy or a slob? Confident or shy as a chipmunk? What kind of music does she like? What does she read? What were her SAT or ACT scores? Can she cook?

When you know how your character would react if she were in a plane crash and several other passengers had also survived, you could write a book about her as long as *War and Peace*, but you will also have to know her that well to decide if she will go to the Colony, even though you will include only a small fraction of what you have discovered about her. What you are looking for is what motivates her. Why does she do what she does, think as she does, feel about herself as she does?

SHOW, DON'T TELL

When you know so much, it is tempting to tell it: My character, Missy, who is a piano tuner and a frump, has long red hair, freckles, skinny legs, hates her sister, and listens to cowboy music.

No. Leave that method to her biographer.

You have to show it without stopping the action of the story:

Missy turned Charlie Black's "I'd Be Better Off Without You" on low before she could face the messages on her answering machine. It could be Cindy. She wondered if her snobby sister even felt the least bit guilty about getting all the family pretty genes and leaving her with red hair, dirty freckles, and legs as skinny as an ostrich. Probably not. With both chairs piled with laundry Missy hadn't gotten around to folding, she sat on the piano bench, but turned her back to the keys. She'd tune the bloody thing one of these days, but after working all day on everyone else's clunkers, she couldn't promise when. Who would she play it for anyway? Sighing, she hit the message button. . . .

CREATING THE PLOT

The plot evolves from *cause and effect.* (We will deal with the concept in more depth in a later chapter.) Something happens that has consequences for your character. The repercussions cause a change to occur. She makes a decision, alters her situation, reverses her luck, tumbles into chaos, or lives happily ever after. (But don't bet on that one. Only Danielle Steel's characters know how to do it.)

It's time to play "what if" again:

What if Missy stomps on the message machine shouting, "You bastard! I loved you, and you ruined my life. I'd like to bury your face in that soufflé . . . as a matter of fact, I think I will." She is laughing as she jumps into the water taxi.

What if Missy turns off the machine and digs through the closet for a scrapbook with a white tulip pressed between the leaves. . . .

What if she digs through the closet for her one good black dress. . . .

By the way, John Turner Harington III is the man at the Colony with the white tulips. What if this were his story?

If the piano tuner and the aristocrat hold no appeal, one of the following might hit your starter button:

STORY STARTERS

☞ What if the doctor said, "Whoops, there seem to be triplets here"?

☞ What if everyone in the class passed the bar except your character?

☞ What if the cruise were a flop until they docked in San Juan?

☞ What if your character were forced to move back home at twenty-eight?

☞ What if your character's widowed mother met a man named Henry and they had sex in her parents' old double bed?

☞ What if the score were tied with four seconds on the clock and Skip passed the ball to your character?

☞ What if the killer left a calling card, the ace of spades?

☞ What if your character infiltrated a militia group operating in the Badlands?

☞ What if your character goes blind?

☞ What if he comes out and his brother tells him he is no longer welcome at any family gathering?

☞ What if that summer your character, expecting a lark, signed up to crew on a luxurious sailboat owned by a wealthy couple from Brazil, but things went bad?

☞ What if your character discovers the fraud, and her boss knows that she knows?

☞ What if your character's wife says, "I want a divorce. I'm going to marry the golf pro at the club"?

☞ What if the judge awarded the kids to your character's husband?

☞ What if your character goes home for Christmas and his mother says, "You're such a nice-looking boy. I wish I had a son"?

☞ What if your character's family do not approve of his fiancée?

☞ What if the FBI asks your character to wear a wire?

☞ What if your character is a doctor and she falls in love with a nurse? (Male or female, it's your call.)

☞ What if your character takes a foster child?

☞ What if your character gets transferred and her husband says, "I won't go with you"?

☞ What if the only person your character ever really loved were gay?

☞ What if the rabbi's (your character) house burned down. He saved the dog, the cat, the Torah, and then went to Tahiti to spend the rest of his life in shorts and sandals?

☞ What if your character spends her wedding night in the emergency room?

☞ What if your character bought a raffle ticket from a kid, not paying any attention to the prize that she won, and it was a spotted horse?

CHAPTER 2

Twice- and Thrice-Told Tales

As we went to press Jane Smiley had won a Pulitzer Prize for turning King Lear into a hog-raising Iowa farmer with a thousand acres. Goneril, Regan, and Cordelia—the farmer's daughters, rechristened Ginny, Rose, and Caroline—hadn't learned a thing from having been through this wrenching plot before. Neither had the farmer. He divided his land and went mad, while the sisters almost drove themselves mad fighting with their old dad, each other, and their husbands.

Before publication of her next novel, I had heard rumors Smiley had taken on one of the comedies. When *Moo* came out and it was about a pig, I at least recognized the mistaken identity theme, but there were so many characters and so many plots and subplots, I felt it was much ado about nothing. I'm still not certain who was Bottom, or if Benedict's and Beatrice's story was in there. I read her other two novels, but if she takes on Hamlet, I think I'll pass. Of course, legend has it Shakespeare never created an original plot. I like Hamlet, Horatio, and Ophelia just the way the Bard presented them, but if you want to read earlier versions, the story is in *Saxo Grammaticus* and Belleforest's *Histoires Tragiques.*

Matteo Bandello (1480–1562) wrote an Italian romance believed to be the original story of star-crossed lovers Romeo and Juliet. Shakespeare penned his version in 1595. For four hundred years their tragic tale has continued to inspire art in many forms, including dance, music, and painting, but especially films like the ever popular *West Side Story.* In 1996, yet another rendition—this one a sexy, violent, almost psychedelic interpretation of the doomed lovers in their rap, car, gun, culture in a seedy Florida beach town—drew large audience.

The Elizabethan writers were obsessed with seeing other worlds through the lens of their own time and place, including the New World, the Americas. They dreamed us into their civilization; now we're dreaming them into ours. Shakespeare's cadences and metaphors, his passions, convictions, and conflicts meet ours in a world of rock, gospel, and shock-pop—all just a CD or radio station away from Mozart and Prokofiev.

Consider the possibilities for a novel. Sins of the fathers destroy the youths' chance for happiness. Further corruption comes from the bawdy nurse who tries to stain Juliet's innocence and purity. Romeo's hotheaded friend Mercutio provides more than enough action to keep the plot moving. There's even a bumbling friar, if you feel the need for another adult foil.

In *Twice upon a Time,* Daniel Stern didn't even bother camouflaging the inspiration for his stories. One is called "A Clean Well-Lighted Place by Ernest Hemingway: A Story." Hemingway's two waiters in a café became, in Stern's story, two men in the movie world—one haunted by the Hemingway story.

Claire Bloom borrowed an Ibsen play title for the overriding ironic metaphor of her autobiography, as well as using an altered version in her own *Leaving a Doll's House.* (In Ibsen's play *A Doll's House* Nora asserts her independence by finally leaving her husband, who treats her like a child.) Bloom's book started brush fires in two countries and sent commentators scurrying to the classics for allusions to water down the damage done to whichever spouse was their hero in this modern, messy marriage. Among others, actress Bloom was called Medea; brooding novelist Philip Roth, Heathcliff. I know our purpose is to focus on fiction, but that is what some critics cheekily called Bloom's book. They were Roth's champions.

New Yorker reviewer Daphne Merkin, a Bloom attacker, said the book had "become a source of lurid fascination—a sort of upscale Lorena Bobbitt [allusion to tabloid current event] for the kaffeeklatsch set." Merkin went on to proclaim Bloom's purpose had been to play the hapless victim of Roth's misogyny, but after sorting out all the actress's dirty linen, the critic decreed her to be badly miscast. Bloom, the critic concludes, is just a stage brat [stock character] who never stopped using men for her own ends. This time, the critic says, she wants revenge.

Roth's bloated ego and his sexually incorrect imagination turned me off about five books back. I have an image of him trying to write while sucking his thumb and holding his psychiatrist's hand, but knowing his habit of using his most intimate relationships as grist for his misogynous tales, if I were Bloom I'd head for a long voyage on a tramp steamer when his next novel is published. (In a later chapter, we will go into the tantalizing hazards of using thinly disguised real people for characters.)

ALLUSIONS LAZILY USED AS SHORTCUTS

The gates have been lowered on poetic license, but so have the reasons for filing lawsuits. I would suggest you stay within the bounds of good taste, especially if you reiterate his work or create a character based on a living author. Saul Bellow got away with using the tormented poet Delmore Schwartz as the model for his main character in *Humboldt's Gift*, but British poet Stephen Spender sued (and won) when David Levitt embroidered scenes in his novel that had been lifted from Spender's autobiography.

If you are serious about developing your skills, imagine your own idiosyncratic poet. Taking a shortcut like alluding to a Sylvia Plath or a Robert Frost demonstrates laziness or a lack of imagination. It's like saying your character has a smile as warm as Richard Nixon's or she looks like Marilyn Monroe, rather than finding the language to describe his thin lips with no give, or the mischief your protagonist's pouty lips have caused.

When a writer like Smiley retells a story such as King Lear's she is tackling universal situations: problems of and for an aging parent, sibling rivalry, and the tangle of inheritance, themes—when handled well—guaranteed to elicit an emotional response because they are and have been pervasive in every generation. But she can't win a Pulitzer by simply saying her character was like Shakespeare's king. Making her protagonist not a leader but a farmer raising hogs, she underscores the universality of the conflict. It's about power—losing it or giving it away; it's about entitlement.

Since most readers have been tempted themselves, they will respond to your story about a character who sells his soul to the devil if you *show* don't *tell* them how Faust falls again. Your character might be Fred, a plumber from Canarsie, who meets a commissioner at City Hall—the one who awards contracts. Or she could be Freda, the manicurist from Flint—who encounters one of her regulars' estranged husband, the one who's willing to pay a bundle for information.

STOCK CHARACTERS AND ARCHETYPES

When you are looking for material, do not confuse stock characters and archetypes.

Stock characters are types who recur repeatedly in a particular literary genre, like the tight-lipped sheriff who lets his gun do the talking in the Western, the fainting female in a sentimental novel, the wicked stepmother in a fairy tale. The Englishman with a monocle, an exaggerated Oxford accent, and a defective sense of humor is a stock stage character in a comedy. Drawing on a familiar type won't wreck your story. It will depend upon how well you re-create and individualize your version. Hamlet, my favorite prince, combines the attributes of the stock hero of revenge tragedy and those of the Elizabethan melancholic man.

C. G. Jung described archetypes as primordial images formed by repeated experiences in the lives of our ancestors, inherited in our collective unconscious. The Fatal Woman, the Ruthless Male Hero, the Exile's Return, the Devil and God are ubiquitous archetype characters in all types of literature.

NOT WHAT YOU EXPECT

Everyone knows the story of Judas. Most of us have met one or two of his clones at summer camp, at the club, at the altar, in the office, in sixth grade, in the bedroom. You could write a story told from his victim's viewpoint, but how to avoid a sense of déjà vu if he already knows how it will end tenders a problem. In this situation, it's best to remember Aristotle's advice that good drama presents a surprise, but upon reflection, one realizes it was inevitable.

Why not tell the tale from Judas's point of view? Think of the possibilities. He could be a decent person who misunderstood the facts, wasn't given all the information he needed, or was duped into betrayal. A naive narrator who simply can't see what everyone else, especially the reader, understands immediately creates dramatic irony. Readers love to feel more intelligent than the characters.

Now flip to the other side. Dostoyevsky enjoyed showing how a truly twisted and evil person thinks. It would not be mixing metaphors for your Judas to be an heir to Raskolnekov's heinous perspective. The two of them went about their skulduggery gleefully.

Before you frame the story, work out Judas's back story to determine why he is the way he is. Did he feel he never got his fair share? Did he grow up being nurtured on propaganda he accepted as truth? Did he have to find a way to endure a dreadful disappointment? Perhaps you believe in bad seeds, people who are born with a warped outlook on life. No matter how distasteful, all you have to do is make your character believable. The reader must be made to feel: yes, unfortunately, this could have happened, and in his case would have.

Edgar Allan Poe's Judas would be mad, but his delusions

would make him slick and sly. Walking through a story in his shoes could be like a prolonged Halloween. Then there is Flem Snopes, Faulkner's disgusting Judas. When he walks through a story, he literally leaves tracks on the rug.

Try a "not what you expect" twist on the Faust story. Imagine a character who has information the state wants. If he sings, his next chorus could be as a member of the heavenly choir. He didn't learn what he knows at Boy Scout camp. Another character wants his silence. This character packs an Uzi. Who represents the state? You could have three possibilities for the character who will play Faust and the one who will play the role of the devil.

In Emily Brontë's novel *Wuthering Heights,* Heathcliff, whom many have called the devil, was the most interesting character. John Milton's Satan also stole the spotlight in *Paradise Lost.* Scholars do not think that is what this religious poet intended, but a rebel always gets the best lines.

Perhaps your memory and your imagination can work together to find a story in one of the following:

STORY STARTERS

☞ Your character was on top, but when he fell, all the king's horses and all the king's men couldn't put Humpty Dumpty back together again.

☞ Your character might have been the Sleeping Beauty, but it wasn't Prince Charming's kiss that woke her up.

☞ Your character married a charming Peter Pan, but the marriage got old when he did not.

☞ Your character did not need to be reminded that she was not in Kansas anymore, but of course he often did.

☞ He was the Big Bad Wolf, and he did huff and puff until he blew your character's house down.

☞ Behind her back, they called your character Mary Magdalene.

☞ After everything else that had gone wrong, when he got fired your character felt like Job.

☞ When your character went to the wedding without an escort, she felt as if she were the only single animal on Noah's ark.

☞ Your character felt as if he were Abel and his brother were Cain.

☞ When her husband didn't believe she had changed, she called him a Doubting Thomas.

☞ Just as Cain got all the good lines in the Bible, your character felt his brother got all their mother's love and attention.

☞ When your character's prodigal son returned home, there was little hope they would live happily ever after.

☞ Your character falls in love with a man whose past was shadier than Gatsby's.

☞ Your character's father was as obsessed with the rabbits that ravaged his garden as Ahab had been with Moby Dick.

☞ Your character worked for a man with a redneck mentality who called Jews Shylock and Afro Americans Sambo.

☞ When your character's mother found out she was living with her lover, she began to embroider a scarlet letter.

☞ Your character admitted he had committed the crime, but he argued that his punishment was too severe.

☞ Your character's younger brother was as beautiful and as naive as Billy Budd.

☞ When your character learned his shocking secret, she felt like Jane Eyre finding a madwoman in Mr. Rochester's attic.

☞ Back in the 'hood, they called him Uncle Tom just because he was successful.

☞ When he moved from Missouri to New York, it looked as if he and Huck Finn had shopped in the same store.

☞ Your character thought she was looking for the right guy, but after a time it felt more as if she were waiting for Godot.

☞ When your character's wife began to behave more and more like his mother, even put on weight in her derrière like Ma, he wanted to poke out his eyes.

☞ When your character knew the truth about her sister's fiancé, but no one in the family would believe her, she felt she should be rechristened Cassandra.

☞ A friend tells your character, at least Antigone got it over with quickly. The sacrifices she has made for her brother have gone on for a lifetime.

☞ Y.C.'s uncle could find more excuses for divorcing his wives than Henry VIII. Reason number five was a lulu, but then so was she.

☞ Your Romeo's father was the Godfather. Juliet's was the D.A.

☞ Juliet's father was a miner in Appalachia. Romeo's father owned the strip mining company.

☞ Romeo's father was the Republican governor of California. Juliet's father was the Democratic mayor of L.A.

☞ Romeo's father went to West Point. Juliet's mother was born in a Japanese internment camp.

CHAPTER 3

Universal Themes and Symbols

The phoenix might not be your favorite mythical symbol—if your shrink or your mother told you to rise from the ashes when you lost the spelling bee for the whole fifth grade, again when the boss fired you, and once more when your lover left you—but rising from misfortune to fly again makes a good story. Readers identify with the theme, especially those of the Nixon generation.

The old bird Ovid described as being nurtured not on seeds and herbs but on tears still holds a high rank in the death-rebirth motif, one pervasive in literature since the beginning of time. One of my favorites is Fitzgerald's subtle thread in the story of Jimmie Gatz, who rose from the natural ash heap of his birth, and reinvented himself to become Jay Gatsby.

Think of the possibilities:

Your character could have run for public office. She wasn't defeated; she was humiliated. But the end was only the beginning. She checked herself into the psych ward and liked it. She didn't have to make any decisions, cook any meals, do the laundry, kiss any babies who needed changing. . . .

Your character takes his wife, his twins, his Tudor on Bay Shore Drive for granted until one day he comes home to an empty house. No bikes in the drive, no chilled martinis, no easy chair, no prime rib in the oven, only a note on the fridge and a FOR SALE sign on the front lawn. Starting over with the character's intention of finding them could take three hundred pages. Rising again to discover what was it within himself that had made them do it could take four hundred.

Prisons provide dramatic launching pads for the phoenix, but an uncomfortable nest in Shaker Heights also has possibilities. A nefarious lawyer who becomes a born-again preacher has promise, too. The tone could be as ironic as Sinclair Lewis's tale about the sexually powered, hypocrite Elmer Gantry, or as sincere as Thomas Hardy's Clym Yeobright, the native who returned from glamorous Paris to preach to the simple people on Egdon Heath. It's always your call.

Earlier, Cervantes' exquisitely drawn Don Quixote de la Mancha had only whetted readers' appetites for more stories about the hopelessly romantic idealist. Every generation, especially ours, has windmills to battle. The Me generation didn't inspire many beyond merchants who sold BMWs or Rolexes and those who bought S&Ls. After the self-centered eighties and nineties, I would bet editors in major publishing houses would like to cross the bridge to the next century with an optimist knight-errant sallying forth to make a better world, no matter how deluded he might be. Perhaps your protagonist would find his Dulcinea, a damsel in distress over the downward trend of the Dow, but for whom the appeal of the chivalric code did not die with King Arthur and Sir Lancelot.

Cervantes wrote a mock-heroic parody, the humor implicit in the theme of a medieval knight in a modern world (the seventeenth century). You could also do a spoof—your Don Quixote could be a comic character selling used cars or teaching seventh-graders, or he could be a sympathetic protagonist who has not (yet?) become as jaded and cynical as his peers.

PHYSICAL DESCRIPTIONS: WHEN TO PROVIDE THEM

Most memorable characters stay with us because of their deeds, their decisions, their language, but Cervantes painted an unforgettable physical picture of an old man (fifty years old was elderly for a man in 1605 when the book was written). One would not have expected him to play the lead in a Broadway musical. He was tall and lean "with cheeks that appeared to be kissing each other on the side of his mouth and a neck a half yard long." Even his horse, Rocinante, formerly a hack, was a bony old nag.

If you go into great detail about your character's appearance, the reader expects her looks to have significance in the plot, as Don Quixote's did. He was a tad long in the tooth to play the hale, hearty, handsome knight one expects. Shakespeare's Falstaff was too fat to be a soldier. Blanche DuBois had passed her prime, except in a pink light. The plot of "The Gift of the Magi" turns upon the description of the wife's long hair. But try to remember if Hemingway's heroes have blond or brown hair, how much they weigh, the color of their eyes. His soldiers, hunters, fishermen, all become John Wayne look-alikes because of their brave actions, their manly decisions. Don't raise the reader's expectations by spending a hundred words describing your character's dimples unless she is going to use them to her advantage or they are another character's weakness. If you must get wordy about your protagonist's eyes, remember there are already more women in novels with eyes like sapphires and emeralds than Tiffany has stones in their display cases.

With a little luck, this book could become your Pandora's box. You open it to find you not only like to write, but you're good at it. In the beginning you only allow yourself to write in the office at lunch time, but the words are flowing, the plot is hot. You're consumed. You lose your day job, but you write a bestseller.

Pandora is the goddess who brings in her box all the gifts of life, which unfortunately also include death and disease—as well as all the wicked temptations and the wild, irrational tendencies of the imagination that have always beset man. When you choose this theme, it invariably creates a dilemma, a powerful writer's tool to increase tension, dramatize the conflict, and develop the character. Your protagonist confronts a situation requiring a choice between unpleasant alternatives. Should Eve eat the apple or survive in ignorant bliss?

Look up odyssey in your dictionary. If the word is listed only once and is capitalized, buy a new dictionary. Yes, Homer did write, or is alleged to have written, the *Odyssey,* an epic poem about Odysseus's wandering after the Trojan War, but he was not the only person to have had an adventurous journey toward enlightenment, for pete's sake. How about Sacajawea, Huck Finn, Ahab, Natty Bumppo, Bret Harte's gold prospectors, the Merry Pranksters, Cleopatra, Conrad's Kurtz, Jim, and Marlow—to name a few from a multitudinous cast?

Don't be put off from tackling an "on the road" story simply because so many exist. The journey—simply a structuring devise—can lead back in time, into the future, to maturity, to self-discovery, or to Mars. In *The Riders,* Australian novelist Tim Winton sends Fred Scully on a love-crazed odyssey from Ireland to the Greek Isles in search of a woman vanished, but the dark journey ends at the underside of the male psyche. In Cormac McCarthy's *All the Pretty Horses,* sixteen-year-old John Grady Cole rides across the border into Mexico and finds a place where dreams are paid for in blood.

Authors often combine the odyssey and the buddy theme. Butch Cassidy and the Sundance Kid, Jack Kerouac and Dean Moriarty, Neal Cassady and Ken Kesey were the descendants of Don Quixote and Sancho, Huck and Jim, Lennie and George. But clever writers have realized all teams don't have to look like the Lone Ranger and Tonto. Innocent children have made good foils. Tim Winton's Scully travels with his young daughter. Barbara Kingsolver's American Indian child, Turtle, who is Taylor Greer's companion in *The Bean Trees,* worked so effectively that Kingsolver continued their travails in a sequel, *Pigs in Heaven.* And who can forget Phoebe, Holden's little sister, who fights unsuccessfully to keep his journey from ending in the psych ward.

Watson has gotten Conan Doyle out of more jams than

Sherlock Holmes has. Creating a "confidant," a character who takes little part in the action but is a close friend of the protagonist and receives his or her confidences and intimate thoughts, allows the author to reveal the thinking and intentions of the hero without the use of asides, soliloquies, or excessive of narrative summary by the narrator. When John, the librarian/mystery writer I work with, grew peevish about my repeatedly saying, "The pacing is tooooo slow," he gave Cleveland, his PI, a friend on the force (not what you expect), reworked the narrative into dialogue, and went zipping on. (As well as an important technical device in most mysteries, a confidant as best friend is a stock character in young adult fiction.)

If Horatio had not served as Hamlet's confidant, how would we have known the fate of Rosencrantz and Guildenstern and what happened to Ophelia while Hamlet was on his odyssey to discovering the guilt of his uncle?

Although Fergie and Di have proven in print that marrying the prince does not mean you will live happily ever after, the *belief* that it will is and has been the most popular literary theme in the known world. An account of the "Cinderella" story exists in every known language from Arabic to Swahili. I can't prove it, but I think the hope that your prince will come along and save you is responsible for more stupid female decisions than any other idea in Western culture. The concert halls could have been filled with conductors and composers in lipstick, hospitals packed with brain surgeons in skirts, a First Gentleman holding the Bible for the President to swear her oath. But instead of a girl in pigtails dissecting her frog in the lab, she was at home primping for the pimply-faced prince who would find his frog's gizzard before taking her to the ball.

Did the feminist movement make this most universal of all universal themes obsolete? Hardly. The pattern is so deeply embedded in the female subconscious that radical surgery couldn't touch it. In the late seventies when Betty Friedan and Gloria Steinem were the nightly news, one of the most popular movies told the story of a poor factory girl who was rescued by a handsome naval officer. This modern-day prince wore his crisp, white, dress uniform, she her overalls, and when he swaggered up to her dye-press machine, picked her up in his arms like a baby, and carried her out to his sports car carriage, no one in the audience even tittered.

If you want to write a romance novel which sells very well, you have your theme. The heroines might have their bodices ripped, but they are all Cinderellas.

The revenge motif is not as pervasive as the Cinderella story, but it has been the starting point for a long history of stories, including Gothic novels, fairy tales, and mysteries. Revenge motivates Brontë's Heathcliff after he loses the woman he loves. Iago "might" have been seeking revenge for Othello's having passed him over for a promotion. Prospero sought revenge upon those who cast him adrift.

Some do not pack away the traditional witch on her broomstick with the other Halloween decorations. In every season they see her sleeping with the President, casting her spell on the board of directors, leading their children astray, distorting the image of the female gender. A few prick her with a pin to see if she bleeds, while others attack her with their pen and ink. One of the most effective ways to take care of your female character is to have another character accuse her of witchcraft (or the modern equivalent). It's hard to prove, but it strikes such a primal chord, after she is wrapped in the web of accusation, it's almost impossible for her to get loose.

Before 1688, four women had been hanged for witchcraft near Boston, but the principal outbreak of persecution took place in 1692 after an epidemic disease, believed to have been caused by witches, spread through a part of Salem. Volumes have been written about the Salem witch trials. Hawthorne's *The Scarlet Letter* and John Updike's *The Witches of Eastwick* have not begun to tap the potential in the archetype of the witch.

Witches and serpents crouch in that same narrow brain cell where fear lives. The serpent won its place as the most ancient phallic symbol, not only because of its shape, but also because it is the most naked of all animals.

Snakes can symbolize fertility when coiled around a person to give generative heat, but they also represent Lust (luxuria), who is depicted with slithering reptiles hanging from her breasts. Other images show the devil disguised as having the upper half of a female form with an apple of temptation in her mouth and the lower half of a serpent.

Clytemnestra dreamed she gave birth to a snake who suckled her. The soothsayers explained it as her punishment for having incurred the anger of the dead.

No wonder most people fear this creepy creature that has no backbone. If horror is your genre, you could play on that infinite fear.

We read to learn more about ourselves and why the world works as it does. That urge explains why a character type, plot pattern, or description occurs frequently. These universal topics evoke profound emotional responses in the reader who has lost or won similar battles. So when a story works, through the exploration of your character and his activities, you have probed the familiar—the reoccurring conflicts, joys, dreads, terrors, strengths, and weaknesses in the lives of everyman.

What makes a myth has more to do with fantasy than with everyday fact, as our continued fascination with Amelia Earhart—tomboy in a glamour girl body, the great heroine who failed—has proven. She has become a mythical creature because she reflects so many of our fantasies. Jane Mendelsohn, who wrote *I Was Amelia Earhart*, a fictional memoir (whatever that might be), said Earhart was romantic and pragmatic, masculine and feminine. She had a passion for life and a suicidal streak. She wanted to fly because she thought women should do things men had done, but she also wanted to fly for the fun of it.

The continued suspense and tension in her story exists because she disappeared. Is she dead or alive? It's uncanny. We know she is dead, but it feels as if she is alive— the vivid carrier of our dreams. Eternally in flight, she is a symbol of our imagination and still embodies the American dream of freedom.

A word of caution: Don't use silly symbols like flocks of birds symbolizing guardian angels as Andre Brink did in his novel *Imaginings of Sand*. The critics had a field day with it.

With a little luck, one of the following might strike a chord with you:

STORY STARTERS

☞ Your Don Quixote character is a hot dog street vendor who tries to help old ladies, the blind, children, distressed damsels, who don't always want to be helped.

☞ Your Don Quixote starts a far-fetched business. He is convinced it will not only support his family comfortably, but improve the quality of life.

☞ Your Don Quixote thinks if she doesn't criticize and she continues to offer emotional and financial support, her boyfriend will find his way.

☞ Every day your character walked past the place he was forbidden to go. Then one day he opened the door.

☞ Your character was adopted. She had known for a long time where her parents kept the file on her birth mother. Then one day she opened it.

☞ Many of his friends had tried crack, cocaine, heroin, but your character never did. Then one day he pressed the plunger on the syringe.

☞ He had given your character a key but insisted she call before coming over. One night she was in his neighborhood and, on a whim, she stopped by.

☞ When the letter from your character's rebel son/former husband/needy friend/collection agency/old love arrived, your character put it—tightly sealed—in the desk drawer. Then one day she opened it.

☞ The diet and the punishing gym regime had worked. Once again, your character could wear the black velvet pants. As a test of willpower, she kept a gallon of chocolate cherry cordial ice cream in the freezer. It was New Year's Eve. She was alone. She opened the freezer door.

☞ Your character's son refused to let any member of the family into his room. Their agreement worked on the honor system. Then one day he opened the door.

☞ Your character's husband often worked late and had a busy travel schedule. She never checked his stories. Then one night she did.

☞ Your character Emily's odyssey was to the moon. She had four male astronaut fellow travelers. She fell in love with one of them. Use moon puns very, very sparingly.

☞ Your character, Harold, married Wanda, a wonderful woman, who came with a not-so-wonderful eight-year-old daughter called Flame. When, within a few months, Wanda died of cancer, Harold set out across the country to take Flame to live with her grandparents.

☞ Your character, Theo, leaves New York to drive to Santa Fe, where she hopes to try out for a minor role in an opera. Along the way, she picks up Lois, who is running away from Jake, a magician, who has been sawing her in two— literally and figuratively—in front of meager audiences along Route 66.

☞ Your character's company sends him on a business trip with his rival at work. Your character finds a body in the hotel swimming pool. The rival becomes his confidant while he figures out "whodunit."

☞ Your Machiavellian character was no prince, but he knew the moves, especially how to eliminate rivals. He had learned there was no need to use force when fraud would do.

☞ Your character wanted revenge when the coach cut him from the first string.

☞ When Mazie not only rejected him, but laughed at him, your character vowed to get even.

☞ Your character learned he had been disinherited at the reading of his mother's will. It was too late to repay her, but he would take his vengeance on his sister, Mom's favorite.

☞ Your character loved Clarence. He loved her. But Clarence's mother thought your character was using witchcraft to alienate her only son from his mother.

☞ When your character was a child, she and her friends thought a witch lived in the house on Devil's Lane. The woman had a black cat, kept her shades drawn, and some said she had two thumbs and could take off warts with spit.

CHAPTER 4

Overheard and Observed

On Wednesday, *The New York Times* runs a column called the "Metropolitan Diary." The piece resembles a writer's notebook. People submit anecdotes, silly things they have seen, or funny conversations they have overheard. There is a story trapped in most entries, just as there will be in your notebook when you begin to think like a writer.

For example, on Halloween someone saw a mother trying to corral children at the parade. She was asked where her costume was. "I have it on," she says. "I'm a Mother." What was her tone, the expression on her face? Is she going to take these kids home to give them hugs, milk, and cookies, or is she going to abandon them and her costume at the bus stop and head for Las Vegas? By the time you write the story, unless there was something as unusual about her appearance as Don Quixote's long neck, you probably won't remember what she looked like, what her Mother's costume was. That's okay. Your mother could have straggly hair, skin so white the blue veins show at her temples.

Make her flat-chested like a young boy. In the ladies' room at the bus station she could open a Woolworth's shopping bag that contains a package of hot rollers, a padded bra, a package of black fishnet stockings, a bottle of suntan bronzing makeup, and a faux leopard-skin teddy. . . . Hold that image; there might be a story there.

Many of the "Metropolitan Diary" accounts poke fun at provincialism, a chronic disease of epidemic proportions for New Yorkers, but a source of fun for a story. Here is an incident I have stashed in my notebook for further use. (Keep in mind, more than twenty years ago I emigrated from Chicago to the East Side.)

Recently, I was invited to be a guest at a long-established fiction writer's group that had lost one of its regulars. I ask writers in my "So You Want to Write a Novel" course at the New School to read their work to peers, but this was *my* first experience at personally testing the value of this practice.

The setting for my work was Chicago, with a flashback to the protagonist's back story on a farm in Southern Illinois. The conflict lay with her husband, the CEO of a Fortune 500 company whose power affected Washington, Wall Street, and my character.

I began with reservations, but my confidence soared as the other writers leaned forward. I increased the volume slightly, but in such a small room, I assumed, interest not lack of understanding explained their postures.

Silence followed my finish. Then one of the usually articulate listeners, obviously struggling for words, said, "It was so . . . so American."

"Yes," the others chimed in, "So very American."

"American, like *Babbitt*," one said. "I haven't read it since it was assigned at Barnard, but as I recall . . . this was like *Babbitt* . . . so American."

I looked out the window onto West Seventy-second Street to see kids chasing one another around trees in the park, women lugging grocery bags, teenagers French-kissing at the bus stop, a man getting a haircut across the street.

"What is this?" I asked gesturing toward the scene out the window.

"Oh, this is the Upper West Side."

This incident waits in my notebook along with those recorded after speaking to another Upper West Side friend. She saw the Midwest as sort of like Midtown, and once called to ask if she could have lunch with my mother in Illinois the day she was making a speech in Omaha. She wanted to meet my mother because she had never known anyone who voted for Richard Nixon.

Another Upper West Side acquaintance who ventured out to the University of Chicago for his education once told me when he got off the plane at O'Hare, he felt as he were seeing America for the first time. Then there is the story, which could be apocryphal, about the little boy saying his prayers the night before he and his parents were moving. He is alleged to have said, "Good-bye, God, we're going to Chicago."

These and other anecdotes are recorded in my notebook under an oxymoron, "Sophisticated Provincialism." You'll find when you have a glimmer of an idea for a story, material will continue to pop up in conversation and scenes will appear out the bus window, until the file in your mind, or the section in your notebook, is so full you know it's time to begin to put together the pieces.

Currently a character, named Naomi, is slowly emerging from my "Sophisticated Provincialism" notes. Naomi is better educated in a bookish sense than in the ways of the world— she's a tad self-satisfied, bordering on being smug. I see her proud of a carefully selected, dowdy wardrobe that does not include a pair of high heels, yet she always takes cabs. She's probably a red diaper baby, but I imagine her parents dropped out of the movement, not because of McCarthy but because of their financial success. The problem is there is no problem. You don't have a story until you have a problem. If the mother at the Halloween parade above takes her children home to read them a story before their naps, that's nice, but it's not a story. If she abandons the kids at the bus station, you and she have a problem. You also have a story.

CONFLICT

Romeo and Juliet had a problem. They were in love. They wanted to get married. Their families were feuding like the Hatfields and McCoys. Shakespeare had his conflict—the struggle that grows out of the interplay of two opposing forces in a plot. Conflict provides the suspense and tension, the element that keeps readers turning pages. Kurt Vonnegut simplified the process. He says create a character, get him in trouble and get him out of it, and you have a novel.

Writers have the following conflict choices: Your character can struggle against the forces of nature as Jack London's characters battled snowstorms, fire, wild animals. She can strive against an antagonist, an enemy such as Iago, Claggart, an ex-husband, the devil in a suit at the office. He might fight against society as Dickens's Pip, David Copperfield, Oliver, and Little Dorrit all did. Like Macbeth, your character could struggle for mastery of conflicting elements within his character. Unless you call upon the gods to intervene, it's best to avoid having a protagonist at war with fate.

To create a conflict for my provincial New Yorker, Naomi has to want something. Someone or something has to stand in her way, making it seem impossible for her to reach her goal. Let's say many of her Barnard/Columbia classmates have become successful: Nancy received the National Book Award, Joseph has a column in *The Times*, Donald bought the Chrysler Building, for pity's sake. Being ambitious and competitive, their success eats her flesh. Then . . . what if someone reads one of her scripts and likes it a lot. The contract tastes like caviar, but . . . whoops . . . did you say relocate to Hollywood? "Of course, I want fame and fortune . . . IN NEW YORK! Who at Columbia can hear me crowing from L.A.?" Naomi has a conflict. I have a story.

The first step for you: Wherever you go—on a plane to Scotland or in a car to the supermarket—listen and watch for your character, your incident. Unless he exists in a hermetically sealed capsule, he will come ready-made with problems and trouble hanging from and clinging to his limbs.

Take this forty-something man who lives on my block. He always wears a sly, secretive smile . . . happy? No, eerie. For fifteen years I've seen him in the park, at the cleaners, at the newsstand. I've never heard him utter a sound. He doesn't speak to anyone in the shops, never strolls with a friend or relative, even during Hanukkah or on Thanksgiving. Every day is a dog show on our street, but he doesn't join the dog walkers. He sprints along with his head cocked, as if he's smiling because someone is telling him an amusing story or singing a favorite song in his ear, but he isn't wired to a Walkman. He glides through our neighborhood visibly invisible. I think he is a character looking for an author.

The man there on the camp stool, the one wearing the expensive leather jacket and cap, the one who is missing three or four upper front teeth, is looking for change. He might once have been a basketball player streaking down the floor, then pulling up for a three-pointer. He's tall enough. But now he works in front of my bank, shaking his paper cup until the quarters rattle. Only the smiler above doesn't hear the jingling coins, meant to jingle our conscience. For a few days a woman with her own cup staked out the end of the block near the bus stop, but she and the man in the leather jacket must have worked out the border dispute diplomatically. She lasted only a few days. If there had been a fracas, one of our doormen would have told me. The tall man still arrives around nine thirty with a carton of Starbucks coffee. In the winter he brings a handsome plaid blanket to wrap up in, but the hours are good. At exactly four-thirty every day he saunters up to the newsstand, buys a late edition of *The Post,* and boards the Q32, the bus that goes across the Fifty-ninth Street Bridge into Queens.

Where does he get off the Q32? Is there someone there to meet him? Why does he work this block? What's his weekly take after he pays for the pricey Starbucks coffee and the three-dollar round-trip fare on the Q32? He has a story. If you can find it, it's yours.

Does someone assign the territories to the people who live off the streets? Do they take a cut? The guys in our area who collect the returnable bottles when they're set on the curb in blue bags on Friday night for Saturday pickup have a supervisor. It's the black cowgirl in the shades with black lenses. She wears tight black pants, a Western shirt, cowboy hat, and boots, and she smokes long, skinny, black cigarettes and taps her foot while her crew does its sorting in the alley near the back door to the coffee shop. They dump their collections into enormous canvas containers on casters, like those at the cleaners and laundry. They work fast and disappear in the dark, leaving no trace.

In my building there is an aristocratic European in her early eighties who rides in custom-made jodhpurs and boots on sunny Saturday mornings. Every Friday, she receives a dozen long-stem red roses with a gift card attached she doesn't have to read. Her Pekinese dog with the sucker-sized, soulful eyes is named Claire. Descended from a breed bred for Chinese royalty, Claire doesn't like to be walked, she likes to be carried, and she hates men, growls at them in the elevator. The lady says Claire is traumatized because she was once raped.

Is it Claire's or the woman's story?

You are welcome to any of the characters and incidents in my neighborhood, but finding them in yours could add some ginger to your life. If you are thinking about writing and you live in a city, I assume you know about one of the most mysterious, but most effective communication systems known to humankind. Doormen. They know all the stories, not only in your building but for blocks around. I never see them talking to one another or picking up the phone, but they have a system. When I got a $135 speeding ticket, for days a doorman on the next block tipped his hat and looked sympathetic. If you don't complain too much about the elevator or the mail being late, and if your Christmas bonus is reasonable, they will tell their tales. The night doorman has the stories noir. A new cast of characters comes out to play when most apartments are dark.

If you live in a small town, make an excuse to sit in the barber shop or to have your hair done. Every farming community has a family-style restaurant with a cook who can make pies fit for a prince. They all know each other and have already exchanged their news, several times. You'll have to be a real Scrooge not to be drawn into the talk. Take your notebook. Truck stops are the best, especially since they now have telephones in all the booths. It's all right to eavesdrop. That's what writers do. Where do you think Nicholas Evans, who wrote *The Horse Whisperer*, got the idea for that big rig wreck that drove his plot for four hundred pages?

I'm thinking about a story with a trucker as the protago-

nist because I'm curious about those beds built into the
cabs. I've heard that space is like a can of condensed luxury with TV and bath. I've also heard the bed can accom-
modate two if you like to cuddle. If I decide to write the
story, in the name of research I could ask for a peek into
one of those big shiny brutes—the ones with more chrome
pipes and paraphernalia than a church organ.

If writing an "on the road in a big rig" tale appeals to
you, too, feel free. We could not write the same story if we
were twins and trying. (In a later chapter we will talk about
how voice and tone alter material.)

If you ride the subway, the bus, or the commuter train,
and you can't find a story starter, sorry, but I'm afraid
you're not paying attention. Wall Street straphangers all
look alike, or maybe it's the gray suits, blue oxford-cloth
shirts, and red suspenders that make them appear to be
a chain of paper dolls, but their dialogue is dynamite. It's
tense, it's terse, it's Armageddon, it's the World Series, it's
Super Bowl Sunday:

"After TWA 800, there's got to be an end run around
transportations, or it's the whole ball game." "Yeah, but
don't forget *The Journal* bombed GE and even took a potshot at utilities, for chrissakes." "Merrill will go down on
this one, but that Hun in a petticoat at Shearson called it
right. Smells like insider shit." "She's gonna strike out. Her
bond scare was a fly ball. And Smith Barney's gunning
for her."

Sort out the mixed metaphors, like you pick the cashews
out of a bowl of nuts at the bar. Then imagine a back story
for one of them. Did life begin at Princeton or Peoria?
What's the balance in his checking account? Is the chap
on the next strap his confidant or his antagonist? If you
still haven't found his problem, check his medical records.
How did his stress test read? Does the firm demand a drug
test? AIDS? You could zoom in to let the reader see the
tiny hole in his earlobe. He would, of course, never wear
the skull-and-crossbones earring to the office. The chairman is a notorious homophobe.

Currently, another gaggle of those guys in gray suits,
having hired someone to take their broker's test, are wearing handcuffs just below their Rolex watches. The man who

took the exams for $5,000 per pop intrigues me. Give him a back story, find his motivation, and he is yours.

If trees could talk, think of the tales those that grow above a park bench could tell. Couples break up, make up, and make out on park benches. Old men in bedroom slippers remember the good old days. Children chip their teeth, break their arms and their mother's hearts. Sometimes the bench by the pond is where a child meets Dad when it's his week for visitation rights. He can't come to the house. Mom's not speaking to him. Besides he doesn't want to see her. He's three weeks behind with his childcare payments. That bench, a bit secluded by the bushes, is where the gang who attacked the two joggers is alleged to have sat, casually waiting for their prey.

Further down the path by the waterfall, see the woman in the big floppy hat with yards of veil—the one who comes every day. The hat protects her from the sun and mosquitoes. And from recognition, some say. A well-known poet? A famous actress? The former mistress to a President? The regulars can't agree, but once she was somebody. Truman Capote would have loved this character. Her beauty is there, just faded like an old lacy valentine. Children adore her. Perhaps because she never lost her sense of wonder. Perhaps because she is a wee bit eccentric—charmingly strange, not scary. The children would have chocolate peanut butter cups for breakfast and nibble at some of the seeds meant for the birds, if their mothers would let them. Capote and Tennessee Williams are both dead, so you might want to give her a story. She deserves it.

Take your notebook to the supermarket. Characters wander up and down every aisle—the one with such exquisite taste she spends fifty dollars and can tuck her bag into her tote—as well as the one who times her daily arrival with the butcher's setting out chunks of hot sausage and a box of toothpicks. If the deli man cuts a new bread, or especially a cake, into small pieces, she has a very tasty lunch. But the character who intrigues me most works on the checkout line. She hates her job and me. I try not to take it personally. She hates all the other shoppers, too. At first I thought she might be deaf, but once when I asked her why she was so grumpy, she answered, "I have a headache. You would, too, if you had to spend your life here. I only go home to sleep." She has a problem, but any solution I imagine is so grim, I don't have the heart to tackle it. I know I would write her out of my grocery store, but she would probably find a reason to hate working at Tiffany's, too.

Look and listen for gems from your friends and family, but don't overlook bits of dialogue overheard out of context, too good not to be put in a character's mouth, like, "I used to make my brother eat bugs. He liked them," or "I didn't really want to marry Jerrod, but he said he'd kill himself if I didn't, so I did."

Until you find something intriguing—and you will—one of the following might lead you down the right road:

STORY STARTERS

☞ Every day your character, the patient nanny, brought the spoiled four-year-old to the playground in the park. He kicked and bit the other children and sometimes the nanny. Parents and other nannies complained when he threw sand, toys, and tantrums. She tried discipline, sweet talk, and bribes. One day he threw their lunch in the fountain, broke her glasses, and called her an ugly old frog. She started to spank him and shake him and couldn't stop. The policeman on the beat arrested her.

☞ Your character's name is Hope. She moved to the city from Tennessee. She's homesick and broke when she meets a man in the park who promises to solve all her problems.

☞ Your character's name is Chance. He has been unfairly fired. If he had some capital, he could start his consulting business and marry Kathy. A man flies past him, tosses a bag in the bushes. Three policeman round the bend in hot pursuit. After they pass, Chance opens the bag filled with many hundred-dollar bills.

☞ Every day after school, your character, the kid with hoop dreams, shoots baskets in the park. One day he sees an NBA star feeding peanuts to the squirrels.

☞ Your character came to the park to sketch. She often tried to catch the essence of the man who ate his lunch on the same bench every day, even when it was cold. When she felt she had captured it, she fell in love with him . . . or her sketch of him.

☞ Someone left the door unlatched in the monkey cage at the zoo. A spider monkey hopped up on the bench beside your character. He sat for a moment before he threw his arms around her neck and would not let go.

☞ Your character always read the paper on the commuter train, but one morning the paper was late. He was watching the people who got off three stops before his. He saw her just as the doors closed and his train skimmed on down the tracks.

☞ "Your mother died early this morning," the night nurse at the hospital said. Your character hung up the phone before saying, "Good."

☞ In the corridor of the divorce court your character screamed, "If you don't stop this nonsense, I'll kill you." Then someone did.

☞ Your character remembers well the day his seven-year-old son said, very quietly, "You are a phony."

☞ Your character found the note on the fridge. It said, "Your brother and I have fallen in love. We are going to Alaska. I am sorry."

☞ "I sold your horse," your character's father said.

☞ When the minister asked if anyone knew any reason why these people should not be joined in holy matrimony, Y.C.—the bride—heard the guest shuffling about to get a good look. Then she heard his voice.

☞ "I didn't mean for it to happen, but I've fallen in love with someone else." Your character had been married to him for seventeen years.

☞ Your character refused to open the registered letter. She knew what was in it.

☞ Your character was waiting at a crowded bus stop when the car went out of control.

☞ His father had always told your character he would never amount to a damn. That was before he was awarded the Medal of Honor.

☞ With a brave smile, your character slapped a plastic card onto the hideous dinner bill. The smile turned to a goofy grin when the waiter returned the first card, which wouldn't work. He didn't panic until the third one was rejected.

☞ Your character had a history of obsessive behavior before she developed a passion for. . . .

☞ That can't be my child the teacher is describing, your character thinks as she squirms in the chair too small for her.

☞ INSUFFICIENT FUNDS was stamped in red across the check, as if your character had to be reminded.

☞ "Sure I want your job, and I'll get it, too," he had said to your character at the Christmas party. Of course he had been drunk, but some weird things had been happening at the office.

☞ "Of course he's crooked, but they all are. How else do you get power in this office/county/country?" Your character realized they were talking about him.

☞ "You have the intellectual heft of a cotton ball," your character's professor said.

☞ "I wish you had been my brother, but I'm sorry you're my husband," she told your character.

☞ At your character's first gallery opening, she listened as people discussed her and her work. The next day she went to bartending school.

☞ "I'll change after we're married. Really. Just a few wild oats, okay? What's the big deal? I'm gonna change, no kidding," he said to your character.

☞ Your character hated to borrow money from her. Not that she wouldn't loan it to him, but she so enjoyed his having to ask her, of all people.

☞ "You have glued yourself to the wrong side of this culture," the immigrant mother, your character, said when she bailed her child out of jail once again.

☞ "Cow!" Your character's vegetarian lunch companion screeched, holding a hunk of beef between his chopsticks.

CHAPTER 5

Current Events

Here is my best advice to *fiction* writers: Make it up.

In workshops when a scene isn't working, a character is as dry as yesterday's toast, or as incredible as Spider Man, too often the writer will look at me with eyes as big as shooter marbles and say—sometimes indignantly, "But that's the way it really happened," or "That's the way she actually behaved." Worst of all is, "I saw her on the telly/ read about her in the paper." When a storyteller writes about real people involved in headline stories, he has elected journalists and daytime talk-show hosts to be his unlikely muse. Don't be lured into the trap of writing about the President, Ivana Trump, and especially O.J. Simpson.

Actual murder trials have always tempted novelists. A few—written before cases began to be tried on TV as well as in courtroom—like Stendhal's *The Red and the Black*, Dostoyevsky's *Crime and Punishment* and Dreiser's *An American Tragedy*—have been masterpieces, but more have failed or fallen short.

One of the more spectacular cases happened in 1924. Nathan Leopold and Richard Loeb, sons of two wealthy and respected Chicago families, murdered Bobby Frank, the young son of another prominent South Side family. Everyone had expected greatness from these boys with IQs far above average, but instead they applied their intelligence to planning to kill just for the thrill of it, just to prove they were smart enough to get away with it. Especially intriguing was Loeb, the mastermind alleged to have used his charismatic power to persuade Leopold, his devoted admirer. Loeb seemed like a character created by Dostoyevsky or Poe. Clarence Darrow, the noted trial lawyer, presented a remarkable temporary insanity defense that kept the young men out of the gas chamber, but which did not satisfy the public's curiosity about the "thrill" murder trial. Close to a century later, sociologists, psychiatrists, and fiction writers still have not solved the case.

In 1956 Meyer Levin wrote *Compulsion,* a novel based on the Leopold and Loeb case. In a foreword he said:

> If I have followed an actual case, are these, then, actual persons? Here I would avoid the modern novelist's conventional disclaimer, which no one fully believes in any case. I follow known events. Some scenes are, however, total interpolations, and some of my personages have no correspondence to persons in the case in questions. This will be recognized as the method of the historical novel. I suppose *Compulsion* may be called a contemporary historical novel or a documentary novel, as distinct from a roman à clef.

The author doth protest too much. When you have to create an oxymoron to categorize what is supposed to be a novel (an extended fictional prose narrative), you have a problem, and it's not the conflict of your story. It's difficult to please anyone—especially yourself, I would think—when you write "kind of," "sort of," "maybe," a novel. In the Leopold and Loeb case, there were volumes of peripheral information, much of it biased, and too many theories about motivation. In my opinion this is too cramped a box for a writer's imagination.

Loeb died in prison, perhaps murdered as a result of a homosexual situation gone wrong. Late in his life, Leopold was paroled. He married, took an assumed name, lived offshore of the United States and, according to my friend who knew him, lived a life of service. Their real story is still unknown.

Meyer Levin had a theory that certain crimes seem to epitomize the thinking of their era. If he is right, the 1995 O.J. Simpson murder trial issued a wake-up call to the diversity in our society, but I hope it has not inspired anyone reading this book to write a novel. As we go to print, seventy-two (and counting) books about the tragic event have been published. If there is a masterpiece among them, I haven't heard. I expected some far-out and even distasteful manuscripts to slide across editors' transoms, but thought surely no one would attempt to give Nicole's dog's eye-witness account. Wrong. I know an editor who got one.

INHERENT DANGERS IN USING REAL-LIFE EVENTS

A didactic work is designed to demonstrate, or to present in a persuasive form, a moral, religious, thesis or doctrine. Didactic works differ from imaginative works, which are written not to enforce a belief but as ends in themselves. Milton's *Paradise Lost*, however, is didactic, as are many great literary masterpieces.

Propaganda is reserved for that species of didactic work that undertakes to move the reader to take a position on an issue. Harriet Beecher Stowe's *Uncle Tom's Cabin*, Upton Sinclair's *The Jungle*, and George Orwell's *1984* are propagandistic. They are remembered not as great works of fiction but for the doctrines they preached so effectively.

The Simpson defense lawyers played the race card and got away with it, but you probably wouldn't in a novel, no matter which side you took. If you want to moralize, write a letter to the editor, organize a protest march, find a pulpit and give a sermon. If you want to write a novel about the problems in a mixed marriage, the price of fame, biased law enforcement, or a murder mystery, create your own situation, your own characters. Only people in a coma will not know how the O.J. cases have turned out. How would you create suspense?

When you write a murder mystery, I suggest you probe

your own experience—what you see and hear. Trust your instincts. Give your imagination a chance to soar rather than using secondhand imaginings from reporters and lawyers.

When a case plays on your TV, listen to the lawyers' language, watch jury behavior, note how far reporters will go for a story such as the one who asked Patty Hearst what she was wearing when her kidnapper raped her. Apply what you see and hear to a trail you create, one in which you can understand the motive, play judge and jury. Better material lies in treating grotesque and outlandish events in a generic sense. This is especially true in an age when television has already shown all episodes of the serialized plot and allowed lawyers to present character sketches of defendant and victims the mothers of those involved could not recognize.

INHERENT DANGERS IN USING REAL-LIFE PEOPLE

Good taste, legal fees, and displaying a lack of imagination should deter serious writers from plagiarizing a real person's life, especially their own. Lack of discretion and the cost of a defamation of character suit need no explanation, but the pitfalls of casting real people as fictional characters does.

Not only the literary world snickered when Donald Trump's wife, Ivana, "supposedly" wrote a "novel" after he had a highly publicized affair with a younger model, Marla Maples, and left Ivana. Even the staid *Wall Street Journal* chuckled ironically at both Trumps. Reviewer Lee Lescaze said—in addition to a fondness for plastic surgery—Ivana had a liking for self-promotion and a fascination with herself she thought we should share. The wealth acquired through divorce from the famous husband who discarded her gave Ivana access to a clutch of editors, publishers, and ghost-writers, who have enabled her to produce a book that offers "a lesson in the uses of fiction and the price of silence." In comparison to other costly settlements like Norman Lear's, Lescaze calls Ivana's settlement of millions "a low-rent divorce" and said The Donald should know you get what you pay for and silence doesn't come cheap.

Camille Marchetta received $350,000 and bad reviews for writing *All for Love.* Ivana received three million for having lived it. Lescaze's review ends with a warning for writers and lovers: "More and more marriages protect property with prenuptial agreements. But in the matter of post-marital intellectual property, who is protecting the public?"

Maybe Pete Hammill, who became the editor in chief of *The Daily News* in 1996. At his first editorial meeting, he gave advice I thought would work for fiction writers, too:

"*The News* must . . . de-emphasize pseudo-celebrities who have become such tabloid staples that you might actually believe Joey Buttafuoco is an actor. That goes for perennials like Ivana Trump too.

"We should never look like we're pressing our nose to the glass, watching the goings-on of the privileged . . . saying, 'Oh gee, I wish I had Ivana's yacht.' Most people in this city laugh at these people."

No one was protecting the public's intelligence after the Watergate scandal. Hordes took shots at President Nixon and called it fiction that no one any longer remembers. However, *Primary Colors,* a thinly disguised tale about President Clinton's nefarious means of becoming "The Comeback Kid" in his first campaign, will probably stay in print, at least as long as he stays in the White House. The novel is better written than most of the political payback stories, but the notoriety of the author, "Anonymous," created more interest than the book's literary merits. Almost everyone who had ever known the Clintons—and some who hadn't—received their five minutes of fame, denying they had penned the exposé. *Newsweek*'s Joe Klein disavowed authorship right up to the moment his daughter went to school bragging that her daddy was suddenly rich. For several weeks, editors around the country beat their breasts about Klein's having lost his credibility as a reporter. *Newsweek* did fire him, but *The New Yorker* picked him up before he had to file for unemployment compensation.

Klein might need the money. In 1996, a librarian and literacy teacher filed a hundred-million-dollar libel suit against him. The woman claims that she is the basis for the librarian character in the novel who is supposed to have had a sexual fling with the presidential candidate.

In a review of Meyer Levin's *Compulsion,* Erle Stanley Gardner wrote:

> Since this is a novel Mr. Levin has used fictitious names throughout, yet he follows the established facts of the Loeb-Leopold case so closely that any libelous statement would still be actionable. Probably he has in mind the doctrine of invasion of privacy as far as the family is concerned.

As we go to press, Hollywood has been making many popular movies based on refashioned real-life bad guys who have had their share of media attention. The revisionist-historical figures are villains like corrupt, power-hungry Evita Perón, who has been repackaged into a virtuous champion of the poor; a German spy, who did it only for the love of a woman; hustler Larry Flynt, a pornographic publisher who is depicted as the defender of the First Amendment. Americans have always been fascinated by characters like Jesse James, Belle Starr, Bonnie and Clyde, Al Capone, who showed a sense of rugged individualism, even if they were on the wrong side of the law.

Considering our history, the appeal of the rebel isn't difficult to understand. The original thirteen colonies rebelled against the law and were right, but we become confused about the difference between heroic individuality, which makes possible a greater social freedom, and anarchic individuality, which is ruthless, narcissistic, amoral, and dangerous.

A lesson for writers can be wrung out of this. Create your own characters, but if you can imagine a rebel who is only 50 percent bad, you will not only have readers, but they will keep her alive trying to find a way to defend her deleterious side.

In spite of all the above, the media can provide a wealth of ideas to stimulate your imagination, if used only like yeast—a starter to make your story puff up. In today's paper, I saw several articles with potential:

I found "The Bully Gets Bullied, and the Underdog Reigns," on the sports page. Someone hot-wired a backhoe and mowed down three enormous trees growing on the Great Lawn in Central Park.

Actually, the bully boxer is a household name, but everyone already knows more than most care to know about his tawdry life. Creating your own bully is a snap. All you have to do is remember the one who made your life miserable in sixth grade, in the locker room at U. High, on the task force at your first job. Did he stand with his hands on his hips, with his arms folded over his chest in a three-piece suit, or with his thumbs hooked in his back pockets? There's usually something menacing about a bully's chin.

Just for the fun of it, you might go for a "not what you expect" angle. Make your bully a big lovable lug of a guy from the North Woods, one who doesn't have a bully's heart, until someone laughs at him. But then his mind turns black, and his hands are lethal weapons.

I see a wisp of a girl hot-wiring the backhoe—one with a tongue that must have learned to talk on the docks.

Another story is about a group of nuns, who donated the Christmas tree to Rockefeller Center, and who are really going to miss it. Want to bet one of those nuns didn't agree with Mother Superior when she gave away their tree? I'd write her story as an interior monologue. She'd be the type who sees most everything as a personal slight.

My favorite headline was short, but came with a built-in conflict. "Bad Cop," it said over a picture of a whale of a young guy in leg irons. I put the headline in my notebook but didn't save the picture. He looked so miserable, I would have felt sorry for him and probably have written one of those "crooks with a heart of gold" clichéd tales. At first I thought he had a son upstairs asleep and he was praying the boy didn't wake up to see him being taken away in shackles. But I think a kid sister would be a better twist. Maybe the bad cop still lived at home. He had only one sibling, this girl twelve years younger who bragged and bragged about her hero—her big brother the cop—until one night she saw him shake down a drug runner and put the bag of white powder in his uniform pocket. Did she tell? Or did not telling nearly drive her crazy?

Of course the guy could have married his high school sweetheart, the bouncy cheerleader who had joined the crowd screaming for him, the star tackle, to kill the bums, bust their chops, break their legs. She could be the one sleeping in that upstairs bedroom.

Write it the way it intrigues you. One of the delights of being a writer is being in charge.

I compiled the following jump-starts on the first cold day of the year. My winter coat was still at the cleaners. I found things that suggested them in newspapers and magazines on my desk without ever getting out of my warm robe. Some ideas jumped out of ads, a few from feature stories. The photographs were telling, and the society page always has stories begging to be told. Unfortunately, there are always enough murder mysteries for a series.

STORY STARTERS

☞ The maids at the Waldorf loved your character, in town to receive an award. She made her own bed.

☞ Your character left his deputy position after being passed over for the top job. He wasn't going to report to a woman half his size and half his age.

☞ Your character, a young boy, had searched for leads about the identity of his father in his mother's photo album, and in letters and papers she kept in a file cabinet. Then one day she told him she had been artificially inseminated.

☞ Two feet of wet snow fell while your character's baby took his nap. The lines snapped and the electric power went out at seven. Ten more inches knocked out the phone line. Her Toyota did not have four-wheel drive.

☞ Your character, the victim of a napalm bomb when she was child in Vietnam, comes to Washington, D.C. After dark, when the crowds are gone, she goes to the Vietnam Veterans Memorial, and she remembers. . . .

☞ When lawsuits began to be filed to reclaim Swiss bank accounts opened by those who would become victims of the Holocaust, the problem was that no one had account numbers. Your character found her grandfather's.

☞ Your character had a dream. She wanted to make the maiden voyage on the largest, most luxurious cruise ship to take to the seas. She scrimped and saved for the ticket and part of her wardrobe. The rest she took from savings. Her plane was late landing in New York. Her luggage had been lost. If she were willing to go without her bags she could still make the sailing.

☞ Your character had friends in very high places, more money than anyone needed, a family that thought he was invincible. Then he made a mistake.

☞ A plane crashed. Your character's mistress was on the plane. She had been on her way to tell his wife, his boss, and anyone else who would listen, like reporters. . . .

☞ He was famous. Your character was in Las Vegas for the weekend. They met. On a whim they got married.

☞ There was an airfare war. Just for the heck of it, your character bought a ticket to Barcelona. She had never flown. She had never before crossed the Idaho state line.

☞ Your character, an actor, had a best friend, Sam, who was a director. Sam cast your character as the male lead in a romantic story. He cast Joni, the love of his life, to play the female role. Sam directed them to fall in love, and they did.

☞ Your character said "date rape." He said they had been fooling around after a few beers, and she said yes.

☞ Your character spent twenty years in the diplomatic corps. Having to flatter people all day had made him immune to compliments. His career had sickened him on smoked salmon. Champagne now gave him a headache. One day he took his top hat and applied for a job driving a horse and carriage in the park where he could sit with his back to the people.

☞ Your character looked forward to deer season, like a kid impatient for Christmas. This year, out early on a crisp, frosty morning, he got his prey in his sights and pulled the trigger. A horrifying scream. Oh my god, it was a kid in a brown jacket with a hood.

☞ Your character felt you should get a warning when your luck was about to run out. She had everything: a beautiful home, a handsome husband, a sweet child, many friends. It all changed when, by a fluke, she overheard a conversation in the ladies' room.

☞ Your character had come up the hard way. His fiancée was in the stands. He had played in four other major league games. He came up to bat against a pitcher famous for his hard ball. It hit his knee. Your character heard the bone crack.

☞ The IRS agent checked his tax returns. He just knew both the governor and mayor were crooks. He had a crummy job. Welfare cheats lived better. Your character headed west. He joined the Montana Minutemen.

☞ Your character didn't care how old the singer was, and she wouldn't tell. But she could still prowl the stage as sultry as a kid. She sang in a black slip of a dress, worn with unimpeachable authority, and knew how to extend a shapely leg to its most cosmetic advantage. So the roadhouse wasn't on the Great White Way. He had traveled backroads himself. He sent her a drink.

☞ For forty-five years, your character had run a small shop where she sold diminutive, but exquisite objects—old lead crystal bottles, silver carriage clocks, fine porcelain ring trays, delicate lavalieres, Victorian snuff boxes. Then a very large, clumsy man who smoked a smelly pipe began to drop by every afternoon. She thought he might be courting her.

☞ Your character had married her husband before he became successful. She remembered singing lullabies to her son before he had made hit records. After thirty years, she was sick of reflected glory, so she. . . .

☞ Your character refused to believe his father had taken his own life. He went back to his hometown to uncover the real story.

☞ In the middle of the campaign, the senator in your character's district died of a heart attack. His opposition was a crook. Your character had done grassroots work for the party, but had never run for office. The party chairman asked her to jump in. She did. She won. Your story opens the day she is packing to move to Washington.

☞ Your character had joined the army when he was eighteen. Served with distinction for twenty years. He had been married for fifteen of those years. Had a son and a daughter. Now some raw recruit was accusing him of sexual harassment. A slip of a girl with come-on eyes.

☞ Your character worked a crummy job in the steel mill to put his wife through medical school. They had a deal. When she began to practice, it was supposed to be his turn. He wanted to start a geranium farm. Soon after she hung out her shingle, she went to a medical conference in another city. When she came home, she told her husband she had fallen in love with a surgeon. She wanted a divorce. Her husband just didn't fit into her lifestyle any longer.

☞ Your character, a good Joe, had to get to the airport by five-thirty P.M. to meet his fiancée's plane. He had been working such long hours, she was convinced he was having an affair, which he wasn't. Meeting the flight was a test. If he didn't make it, she was breaking the engagement. The boss kept him in a meeting. He dashed to the street. Cabs were changing shifts. Desperate, he jumps into a car left running in front of a pizza parlor. He plans to leave the car in plain sight at the airport, maybe call the owner if he can find some identification. Then he hears something in the backseat . . . a ten-month-old baby in a pink snowsuit begins to wail.

☞ Your character knew his buddy and teammate was on something again. The manager had said one more chance—this was it. The first game of the series was scheduled for Friday. The team had a better chance with him playing. Your character had a better chance for attention if he weren't. . . .

☞ Your character's father had been a notorious household word—the Godfather to a Mafia family, or a union president on the take, or a political boss who had ruled a large city for years, or a despot who had ruled an entire country. People from Appalachia to Annapolis recognized the family name. Your character's father had been dead or in prison for years when the call came for your character to try to seize the legacy. Write it straight from the point of view of a son who had learned his father's moves or a "not what you expect" take from an heir who is female and meaner than a snake, or from a good guy/good gal perspective whose goal is the cleanse the family's image.

☞ Your character married her husband when they were both outstanding students in law school/medical school/graduate school. He has become well known in the field. His success has made it difficult for her. Explore how the situation has affected their personal life.

CHAPTER 6

Omnipresent Family Affiliations

In a much quoted opening line of *Anna Karenina,* Tolstoy said, "All happy families are like one another; each unhappy family is unhappy in its own way."

Unhappy families began with Adam and Eve, who had two sons, Cain and Abel. Cain, indeed, was not his brother's keeper. In Genesis, we find the first case of sibling rivalry, the first murder, the first kid who talks back. Most writers have been modeling their families on the first family ever since. You will probably have more fun and write more interesting stories if you do, too.

With the exception of Jane Austen's Woodhouses, Elliots, and Bennets, unhappy families like the Karamazovs and the Labdacus (house of the Oedipus legend) make for better stories because they have more conflicts, tension, and suspense. Of course, another writer could have seen at least pain and suffering, if not tragedy, in the life of Austen's middle-class, provincial people, where not much ever happened. But in an Austen story a disastrous event is a woman not finding the husband she wants, or not being invited to a party given by an important host. She presents lives in which there is good breeding, and wit, and sufficient hope of a reasonably satisfactory outcome of whatever difficulties may intrude.

Faulkner's families never live happily ever after. The once aristocractic, but degenerating Compsons and Sartorises still suffer from the feudal illusions of the Civil War. They are being ousted and outdone by the Snopeses, unscrupulous newcomers.

Chivalric Quentin Compson's sound and fury signifies nothing when he kills himself because his sister Caddy lost her virginity, but not to him who loved her best. Benjy's sound and fury signifies nothing because it happens only in his (and Faulkner's) mind and can't be told by the idiot brother who loves Caddy, too, but is mute. The mean, money-grubbing Jason's sound and fury signifies nothing but greed. He doesn't love his sister Caddy or give a fig about family honor, but then he represents the New South and is more Snopes than Compson.

In *As I Lay Dying*, a mother watches one son build her coffin outside her bedroom window, while her unwed pregnant daughter watches her and prays her mother will die soon enough for her to get to town in time for an abortion. The son the woman had by the preacher makes the ultimate sacrifice for her husband, the man who is not his father, while his brothers hate him for being the one she loves the most. Faulkner calls this family Bundren, but if there isn't a portrait of a colonel on the wall, they are all Snopeses.

Carolyn Chute created the next generation of Snopes in American literature. They are boozers and brawlers who spend a lot of time in jail. The women spend most of their time pregnant. Chute calls them, and her book, *The Beans of Egypt, Maine*.

Unlike Faulkner's Compsons, Chekhov's idle aristocrats have not yet lost their civil war, but they will. It's the end of the nineteenth century. The three sisters never get to Moscow, of course, and the Ranevsky family does not save their cherry orchard. The coming of changes for the feudal landowning class, cared for by the serfs, the owned class, is represented by the bourgeois Lopakin, who takes the orchard away from the parasitic estate owners and plans to chop it up.

Faulkner's Dilsey, the Compsons' black housekeeper, endures, but Chekhov's old serf, Firs, whose whole life has been dependent on his master and his cherry orchard, lies down to die—the only thing left for him to do.

Freud has focused the lens of many writers' viewfinder on the family.

Virginia Woolf's James Ramsay has an oedipal dream that determines the subject and the structure of his sail to the lighthouse, the wonder he had looked forward to for years. His mother promises they will go "if it's fine tomorrow." James's expedition, like all quests, is competed only after a series of delays, trials, and ordeals. "But it won't be fine," his father's retort—an act of aggression—initially frustrates the expedition.

In *Sons and Lovers* D.H. Lawrence sets the theme of the demanding mother who, having given up the prospect of achieving a true emotional life with her husband, turns to her son and captures his manhood in her possessive love. Paul Morel loves Miriam and she loves him, but the mother's love prevents him from an adequate response. Paul seeks sexual satisfaction in more casual ways, which his mother tolerates because they do not threaten his status as her lover.

MOTIVATION

Paul Morel's mother's motivation for possessing her son rose from her need for love not being satisfied by her husband, whom she felt was not good enough for her. A reader doesn't have to approve of your character's incentive to find her interesting, but he has to understand what drives her.

For a story to work, your character's motivation—the grounds for her actions in her moral nature and personality—must be clear and consistent. The reader might wish she would behave differently, but he has to believe she can't. She may remain static or change, but she can't suddenly begin to act in a way not grounded in her temperament as you have exposed it. She also must be convincing and lifelike. The alien E.T. did not look like anyone we had ever seen, yet traits like his homesickness made him persuasive and real.

Greed and jealousy, powerful motivating forces, have fueled many excellent stories, but shyness has not had its due. Think of the possibilities, especially if you are creating a plot centering on conflicts within a family. Shyness, resulting from social disappointments and rejection, can stultify your character and add complications to every aspect of his life.

The need to control motivates too many people we all know. Writing a story that focuses on the source of that need not only should make good fiction, but could give you more insight into the human condition. Imagine a woman who controls her spouse and his family by never being satisfied. Mimi claims to be a French aristocrat brought up in lavish circumstances in a villa with servants before her family lost their wealth in a noble and dramatic way—perhaps seized during the war. The story may be partially true or a figment of a disappointed woman's fantasy. Her attitude has always been "been there done that/had that," but on a grander scale, of course. For example, her husband's sister, perhaps your character, is so proud of her first fur coat until Mimi says her mother left her a $100,000 chinchilla, but she sold it and gave the money to an animal rights organization. By putting people down, Mimi feels she raises her own status. Until the family sees through her, they scurry around trying to find presents and cook meals that meet her standards, which they never quite achieve. You could have great fun with irony by allowing your character and the reader to come to understand her motives, but Mimi never realizes they're on to her. Or you could make her a sympathetic character by revealing that her bravado comes from the need to hide a past that is too painful or shameful for her to acknowledge.

Conflict and complications will be the easy part when writing about families. Say "sibling rivalry" at a dinner party and watch everyone forget to eat as they relate tales about competitive brothers, jealous sisters, parents' preferences. If you have a few hours, call me up and ask me about my relationship with my father, how his death affected my life, how his life affected my relationships with men. If you don't have my number, call up *any* woman you know. She'll have a story for you. Since I hope you will have a good life as well as find good material, I suggest you find out how the man in your life got on with his mother before you make any important decisions, like marrying the guy.

Faulkner and Lawrence have not said all there is to say about how hazardous mothering is, especially when the children are grown and the relationship is bittersweet, tangled with the nasty complexities of letting go and holding on. Writer Anne Roiphe says motherhood as life's main occupation is a terrible gamble, a quarter in the slot machine, a bet on the ponies, a sure way to end up with nothing to do but look at old scrapbooks and weep.

In the eighties Sue Miller's *The Good Mother* delved into the conflict between two powerful sets of feelings—the erotic and the maternal, but I haven't read the story examining the conflict between the need to succeed and to nurture. I can imagine a nineties character determined not to make her mother's mistakes and finding herself in the terrible muddle of not finding enough time to be a mother *and* to meet the demands of a career requiring long hours and travel.

Try this at a cocktail party. Talk to strangers. Then, take a guess about their placement in their family. I never miss on firstborns, and I'm pretty good at identifying women who don't have brothers. They're the ones who stand tall, always look you in the eye, and make good, independent protagonists.

Twin stories from *Twelfth Night* to the Bobbsey Twins series fascinate me, as you can tell from the exercises below, but I haven't read a contemporary novel on the subject. Maybe you will write it. I promise I will read it.

Here comes another warning about drawing your character from the exact pattern of someone you know and love or know and hate.

If you want to write a tribute to your grandfather or prove to your mother you did marry the right man, or flatter your uncle Harold into rewriting his will in your favor, buy my book on writing memoirs. Keep in mind, your purpose here is to write "fiction." This chapter focuses on probing universal relationships among blood relatives, and telling old stories in a fresh way. Does that mean you can't tap your own experience? Of course not. But if you stick too closely to the real thing, your motivation to please or pay back will most likely create a stereotype.

Write from experience not about it.

You will have a hard enough time convincing your relatives you haven't betrayed them in print when that has not been your intent. For example, everyone who knew my mother thought I had been born lucky and they were right, but it has been a problem in my work. If I portray a mother who is selfish, controlling, or mean-spirited, my phone begins to ring. "How could you?" they screech, and will not listen when I say, "But that character is *not* my mother. I made her up, honest."

Writing a good story takes a long time, and you have to come out of yourself and become the character you are developing. Maybe one of the following is someone whose shoes you would like to wear for a while:

STORY STARTERS

☞ The Jones had a son—just smart as a whip—then a daughter—just as pretty as a picture. Then, by accident she was sure, they had your character.

☞ The Morgans had Suzanne, then Elizabeth. When the third child, your character, was yet another girl, they just called her Johnny after her father, and gave up. Johnny tried hard to live up to expectations.

☞ In the affluent suburb where your character grew up, her older sister was voted the most likely to succeed at school and at home. What she succeeded in doing the summer before college was getting herself pregnant by her equally handsome and popular boyfriend. Your character had always admired her sister, but then one night she overheard the couple planning a hideous, immoral and illegal way of dealing with their problem.

☞ A smart, attractive woman could always find a husband. Your character Lena had already had three, and had kept some résumés on file, just in case she needed them. But a woman only has one father, and hers, she thought, was a jewel. Her husband hated him, of course, but having two men dueling over her only made life more interesting, until one day things got out of hand.

☞ Your character married Steve before she realized his mother had controlled him by withholding love. Consequently, he had a love/hate relationship for all women. His behavior fluctuated between wanting to please and wanting to punish.

☞ Cash, your character, had grown up in a big old Victorian house with lots of gingerbread and bedrooms. They needed the bedrooms for his stern, if not tyrannical, grandmother and mother, his easy-to-push-around father, and his aunt Lolly who never went out but who loved Cash best. Cash was a freshman at the university when he learned—quite by accident—that Lolly was really his mother. But the correct name for the father was on his fraudulent birth certificate.

☞ Paige, your character—the dependable one—was one of the four Baker sisters. Sarah was the student. Connie was the beauty. Pepper had been the rebel. What else had been left? Of course they hadn't seen Pepper for ages; she had run away. Then one night Paige receives a phone call. . . .

☞ Betty Lou and Bonnie Sue, forty-five-year-old twins, had started in high school as part-time checkers at the supermarket. They were still there, scanning in parallel lanes, carrying on a running dialogue with each other, not their customers. They dyed their straggly hair coal black, had big horse teeth, and were skinny as broomsticks. At home, they shared a room, dressed exactly alike—in teenager garb—wore identical rings—that looked as if they had been Crackerjack prizes—on each finger. Behind their back, people said shopping at the store was like going to a double-feature Halloween movie. Then one day the bread man's wife died. He had three children to raise. On his run, he had known the twins for twenty years. He asked one of them—he thought it was Bonnie Sue, but she was wearing a smock over her nameplate—to go to McDonald's for supper.

☞ Your character and her husband conceived twins through in vitro fertilization. One was black. One was white.

☞ The doctor said Cathy and Cindy were identical twins. Cindy, your character, knew he had lied. So they looked alike, but if they *were* identical, wouldn't she be as intelligent as Cathy instead of making C's while her sister pulled down A's with no effort? Now it was time for college. On the basis of their SAT scores, Cathy could go to Harvard and Cindy to the local junior college.

☞ When Brad, your character, went to the divorce lawyer, he said it's this unnatural twin thing. When her twin sister, who lives 600 miles away, cuts her finger, my wife feels it and jumps in the car before the blood starts to flow. She doesn't need me. Even when we make love, I have this awful feeling her sister knows what we're doing and is judging my performance.

☞ Dana, your character, and David didn't go to a progressive elementary school, so no one thought of splitting them up. When Dana said she couldn't breathe if they made her eat lunch on the girls' side or take PE with them, they just let her follow David's schedule. It was easier, and the school was shorthanded. The twins moved to a large city when they started to high school. No amount of pleading would convince the administration to allow Dana to have the same schedule as David.

☞ Allen, your character, had always hated his twin brother. He had a plan to kill him and assume his perfect brother's identity.

☞ Van, your character, was Jodi's first cousin; their mothers were sisters. Van and Jodi fell in love at eleven. They were twenty-one, and not one thing had changed.

☞ Tom, your character, had always admired, but feared, his father. He told his dad he was gay on his twenty-first birthday. His father said, "I don't have a son who is gay."

☞ Your character's grandfather had acquired great wealth. The second and third generations, including your character, were spending it as fast as they could.

☞ The story opens the day your character says to her shrink,

"My father just doesn't like me. He never did, did he?"
"I'm afraid not," the doctor replies.

☞   Your character's father calls him and his sister into the
study to tell them he plans to make his daughter president
and CEO of the family's company.

☞   "You're not good enough for my son, and you already
know it," her future mother-in-law told your character.

☞   Your character ran away to Seattle, where the action was,
when it became obvious his parents loved the poodle more
than their only son.

☞   Your character's sisters were in college when she, the surprise baby, was born. She found having three mothers
more than anyone should have to bear.

☞   The family squabble had happened years ago, before your
character's father's death, but her brother still had nothing
to do with her or her mother. Two days before his birthday,
she thought, What the hell, and sent him a card.

☞   Your character had an affair with her husband while he
was still married to his first wife, mother of his two sons.
She did get pregnant, and he did get a divorce and marry
her. After the dust had settled, she couldn't understand
why his sons refused at least to treat her politely.

☞   To punish him, your character's father had rewritten his
will leaving him a dollar. His mother said her husband had
intended to change it, but he had a heart attack on his
way to work and died on the train platform. The lawyer
and your character's brother said intent could not invalidate
the existing will.

☞   Your character loved her husband and her daughter, but
she knew he was spoiling their child to the point no one
would like her, eventually not even the girl's mother.

☞   His children were a mess, his wife indifferent. One day
your character started to get on the commuter train, but
thought, I don't want to go home. So he didn't.

☞   Your character, an actor, began to be offered mother roles
about the time her teenage daughter came into full beautiful bloom. She tried so hard not to be envious, but it
was impossible.

☞   Your character's child was a musical prodigy. He was determined to whip that talent into a frenzy. His defense was, What if Mozart's father hadn't pushed him?

☞ "My serious sister changed her named from Tracy to Spacey, my mom bought a miniskirt, my dad grew a beard. And me? I left home," your character says.

☞ "She never seems to have forgiven . . . for his early encouragement and help," your character says, or someone says to her.

☞ Your character watches helplessly as her son falls for the self-centered girl. Not only is she using every trick to snag him, but her entire family seems to have come up with a foolproof plan to help her. Entrapment is the way your character sees it.

CHAPTER 7

Animals as Minor Characters

From the moment I signed the contract for this book, I knew I would have to write this chapter, but I dreaded it. Anyone who has read *Moby Dick, The Old Man and the Sea,* and "Little Red Riding Hood" realizes animals make excellent foils. Anyone invited to a dog lover's home realizes people's reaction to pets is character revealing, and anthropomorphism is a word we should all know how to define. Writing funny stories is difficult, but look at what Mark Twain was able to do with a notorious jumping frog. I *had* to include this category. But hardly anyone understands, much less agrees, with my feeling about four-legged creatures.

Oh, I cried every time I read *Black Beauty* and sobbed in chorus when Bambi's mother fell. Once in Maine I called the state police when a fisherman was shooting the seals that were eating the bait out of his weir. In Australia, I had my picture taken with a koala bear, and I would love to have a zebra for my very own. But notice where these animals live.

Here's the problem. I was born on a farm. Spent my formative years there where the people lived inside and the animals lived outside, which made absolutely good sense to me. We had a sheep shed, a hog house, a doghouse for my father's bird dog, a barn for the horses, cows, and cats. It's hard to get all gushy about an old sow who will eat her babies if you don't watch her; and I wasn't mad about Peaches, the Jersey cow who would butt me off the fence if I tried to sit there while my mother milked her.

But I liked most of the animals, except for the chickens. I hated them, with justification I think. When I was two years old, a rooster jumped on my shoulder. He liked to scared me to death flogging and pecking me. Farm kids couldn't be afraid of the animals, so my father, being a practical man, chopped off the rooster's head with an ax and showed me the carcass to assure me he couldn't hurt me anymore. I've never been to a shrink, so I'm not certain if the flogging or the killing is why I'm still afraid of anything with wings. I did not see the movie *The Birds*.

When I grew up and began to live in cities like Chicago, London, and—worst of all—New York, I was in for a shock. Dogs didn't hunt anything and the cats didn't catch mice, but most horrifying of all, they lived in people's houses, slept on their beds, and, god forbid, ate off their dishes. The first time I went to someone's apartment for dinner and found the cat's litter in the bathroom, I had to put my head between my legs until my stomach settled down.

In my building there is a woman alleged to have three birds—one that talks—flying loose in her apartment. We don't visit, and I try very hard not to imagine the bathroom arrangement.

Marjorie Garber, a Harvard professor, wrote a book entitled *Dog Love*. She suggests that dogs' unconditional love for us should be the model for a truly humane society. Critic Andrew Sullivan didn't much like the book, especially the cutesy anecdotes about Garber's dogs. He said that while reading the book he felt as one does when a friend's large hound is mounting one's shin and the owner smiles benignly as if this weren't a gross violation of manners. I would rather write a funny story about visiting someone with an ill-mannered dog than actually visit one, but if you're like Garber—and the entire population of the

British Isles—who believes that dogs can do no wrong, you could write about a grumpy visitor without a sense of humor.

The first time someone spit on my mink coat and called me nasty names, I thought he was nuts. On the farm everything and everyone had a purpose connected with what seemed to be the natural order. Parents loved and pampered their children. We rode the horses when they weren't pulling something; sheared the sheep for wool; ate the pigs, the chickens, and the Angus cows; and milked the Jerseys. Once someone did give me a pop-eyed goldfish and a salamander, both of which swam round and round in a tiny little bowl on the dining room table for a while. My father had thought they were useless in the first place, and then the salamander crawled out of his cramped swimming pool and slithered into my parents' bed. That was the end of Sally, which, with that sissy name, my father had thought was probably neurotic anyway.

When my kid sister was little, she had a monkey fetish. Her friends played with dolls, but Loann had a monkey menagerie—stuffed monkeys like Mugs—until, to impress me, my gentleman caller gave my kid sister a live monkey that fell for me. If you think this is confusing you should have seen what happened at our house the one weekend we had the monkey. He wrapped his spidery arms around my neck like a furry choker with fingers and refused to let go. My sister cried. She wanted to wear the live necklace. If I pried him loose, he pitched a fit. Finally, I hooked the foolish monkey to a leash, looped it around a kitchen chair leg, and fled while he screeched. The idea had been, if I weren't around, he would let my sister play with him. Wrong. He went wild. Grabbing a full cup of coffee, he sprayed the walls, turned over the chair, threw breakfast dishes, and wet on the floor. We gave him back, and my sister went back to playing with Mugs. I never want to spend another minute with that monkey. If you can use a monkey with an obsessive personality, he is yours.

The thought of sleeping with something furry that can't talk still gives me the creeps, but I've adjusted to most of my friends' having animals in their apartments, even become fond of some of them. There are dogs on my block that show more personality than their owners. My favorite is a bulldog that looks more like Winston Churchill than Churchill's son ever did. I could write a story about that stubborn curmudgeon; some days he plants himself in the middle of the sidewalk and not only refuses to go home, but dares his timid owner just to *try* to move him.

In college one of my professors—a young, attractive, single woman—had a scrawny white poodle that hated men. When I graduated, neurotic Toostie was still ruining my teacher's love life. There is definitely a story there.

My father used to play poker with a man who said he would love to go on vacations with my parents, but he and his wife couldn't leave the boys, which was strange since both couples were in their early sixties. Then my father learned the boys were a pair of black cocker spaniels.

Once I was visiting one of my closest friends, the type who takes in strays—lost animals, runaway kids, women going through divorces or having breakdowns. I shouldn't have been surprised when this weird-looking cat joined me while I was trying to brush my teeth. He looked as if he had been put together with spare parts. He was part Maine Coon, which explained the enormous feet and the tail as bushy as a fox. The small, mummylike head, as well as the bad manners, had to be a legacy from an alley cat. He simply would not allow me to finish my task. In desperation, I called for help. All he wanted was a drink, I was told by my friend's teenage daughter. She turned on the faucet, the cat tipped its head and drank from his personal fountain. The teenager gave me a look, as if any sensible person knew cats jumped into the sink when they were thirsty—the sink where people washed their faces.

My short career at playing cupid ended over the cat issue. An intelligent, attractive friend who wasn't seeing anyone and a funny hunk of a college professor seemed like the perfect match to me. She called the morning after their blind date. Her greeting: "He doesn't like cats," said in the same tone one would use to describe a serial killer, a child abuser. I've always wanted to write it, but she's still my friend, so it's yours if you want it.

One of the more successful businesswomen in New York tried desperately, but in vain, to have a child. Then she bought the most beautiful white cat I've ever seen—long, thick hair and sea green eyes. We all realized transference had gone too far, however, when my friend took the kitty to a dinner party and the cat slipped into the kitchen. When we found her she was daintily licking her paws after having devoured half of the poached salmon the hostess had prepared for our meal. My friend laughed. The hostess cried. And we all went to a restaurant for dinner. Everyone was quite relieved when my friend adopted a child. She moved to Europe. I don't know what happened to the cat.

When Paris-bound Flight 800 crashed over the ocean, all the people and Max were killed. Max, a Cairn terrier, the only animal on board, sat in a small kennel underneath Judith Yee's seat. The terrier's West Village trainer said Max was afraid to fly and did not want to go to Paris. It had taken several days to entice him into his traveling kennel, but Yee wouldn't have gone without him. Scrappy, slightly overweight, Max was her best friend and constant companion around the neighborhood. Friends held a memorial service in the dog run Yee had helped to establish. They hung a bone, a picture of Ms. Yee, and bouquets of flowers on the maple tree in the dog park. The trainer thinks there is a "doggie heaven" and that Max is there.

Well-known painter Andrew Wyeth's siblings all dabbled in art, but, according to Andrew's biographer, Carolyn—the rebellious sister—drank too much and became an eccentric slob who kept messy pets and fed them fancy lobster dinners, ordered in.

Here's a story about the most devoted husband I know. He had three job offers in Europe, but couldn't make his choice on the basis of career opportunities. His wife would go with him only if she could take her cat, which she refused to leave in quarantine. They went to the country that would accept animals straight off the plane.

The closest my parents ever came to splitting up was when my father sold Prince. I knew he was an animal, not a person, and I didn't sleep with him, but I loved that horse. If you've read anything I've ever written, you've probably heard that story. It happened when I was eleven, but I can still cry when I think about that big black horse with three white stockings. He would rear up on call. I usually find a way to put Prince into everything I write.

Alice Hoffman's novel *Turtle Moon* doesn't have much to say about turtles, but she uses two tracking dogs to develop a cop and a boy who had the reputation of being the meanest kid in town, since the cop—who used to be the meanest boy in town—grew up. They both have a way with the dogs, especially a vicious one.

In Cormac McCarthy's *The Crossing*, a fierce, cunning she wolf becomes one of his most complicated and fully developed characters. Billy, the protagonist, finally traps her, but he is so moved with admiration for her bravery and intelligence, he half tames the wolf and leads her on a halter down into Mexico where he presumably hopes to release her. McCarthy's ability to avoid sentimentalizing and anthropomorphizing her gives testimony to his art.

Virginia Woolf wrote a spoof novel, *Flush*, told from the viewpoint of a dog whose name gave the book its title.

I had already bought theater tickets to see *Sylvia* before I found out Sylvia was a dog played by a skinny actress with lots of blond hair.

Steve, a writer in one of my workshops, wrote a scene in which a character baked a little girl's cat. He didn't have to say much else about how cruel she was.

Movies often use cruelty to animals to show the beastly side of characters. Even if you haven't seen *The Godfather*, you probably know about the bloody horse's head put in someone's bed to encourage him to see the Corleone point of view. Then there was the spurned lover who boiled the rabbit in *Fatal Attraction*.

I haven't a clue how to write credibly from an animal's point of view, but if I could, I would choose Jace (Just Another Confused Elephant), a rebellious teenager in the Pilanesberg National Park in South Africa; he has a rap sheet for attacking white rhinoceroses and cars filled with tourists. The park rangers say Jace, one of the young elephants moved from an overpopulated park to Pilanesberg, has had no father figure to teach him how to behave. The park now plans to bring in some bucks in a kind of Big Brother program, hoping the older boys will be able to tame down the juvenile delinquents like Jace. If I were to try to assume Jace's viewpoint, I don't think I would appreciate some guy who thought he was a big shot coming in and telling me what to do . . . but I'm not going to tackle it. Jace—the one with the notch in his ear—is there for the taking.

In big cities, where people live in small spaces, even a stuffed elephant would be out of the question. Cats are usually the pet of choice, but if you want to add to your character's intrigue, you might want to give him an unusual, even exotic, animal. George Clooney, movie and TV heartthrob, has a pet pig. I once was more intrigued by a miniature burro than by the man who owned him. I know an artist in Maine who has brown sheep and blue chickens. Honest. My fifth-grade boyfriend gave me a small green snake in a tobacco sack. I thought the boy and the snake were first rate. But my friend's stepson kept a boa which did not add bliss to her marriage with his father.

NAMING YOUR CHARACTER

Raised by a man who always named his bird dogs Sport, I had to read a lot of books before I realized you could call animals things like Toto, Charlotte, and Dumbo. After I discovered General Lee's biography, I wanted all of our horses to be known as Charger, but for some reason he would never tell me, my father called one Bill. Bill was my father's name. I once had a huge white dog (she lived outside) that looked like a barrel of shredded paper. I can't remember why I christened her Bubbles. I called a funny-looking stray that looked like a skunk Mickey, a name I didn't really appreciate until later. My husband's girlfriend, just before me, was named Mickey, and for years his friends slipped and called me by her name. It pleased me to say, "I had a dog named Mickey, but I'm Lou."

If you create an animal for your story, try either for an unusual name or a funny reason for calling a gerbil George. Robespierre called his dog Blount, but absolutely the best dog name ever was Dorothy Parker's Cliché! When I taught at the University of Chicago, all my colleagues' dogs were named Socrates, or at least that's the way I remember it. My friend the opera singer's dogs were named "Norma," "Aïda," "Carmen," according to the tenor of their voices. It was not an original idea, however. Mozart's dog answered to "Lulu."

F.D.R.'s Fala showed some imagination, but Nixon's

Checkers and Bush's Millie were rather pedestrian. A cat named Socks isn't inspiring, but the Clintons showed pizazz when they named their daughter Chelsea.

When my cousin, Jackie, and I were riding horses and playing cowgirl in our pasture, her persona was Dale Evans and mine was Belle Starr. At that time, probably neither of us knew Dale's real name was Frances Butts (Roy's was Leonard Slye and Trigger was actually the racehorse Golden Cloud), but I knew I didn't want to impersonate someone who called her horse Buttermilk. Besides, Dale Evans was known as the "homebody on the range," and Belle Starr led the Younger Gang.

Racehorse names often defy logic, but usually can be pronounced. However, try Flat Fleet Feet, a filly, whose alliterative name has become the bane of racetrack announcers. The day I found her name in the paper, she had beaten Queen Tutta, Miss Golden Circle, Yanks Music, Thunder Achiever, Shoop and Lottsa Talc, and Unbridled's Song.

I know Tiger Woods works some kind of magic on a golfball, but I wonder if the world would have noticed as quickly if his name had been Henry. Deciding what to call your characters—whither they talk or bark—is serious business.

Authors writing for kids have been known to draw readers away from the TV and video games with characters known as Dinky Hocker, Maniac McGee, Hatter Fox, Willy Wonka.

Dickens holds the blue ribbon for memorable names like Pip, Micawber, Chuzzlewit, Dombey, Scrooge, Bumble, Sikes, Tiny Tim, Edwin Drood. No one forgets Emily Brontë's Heathcliff, Shakespeare's Falstaff, Tennyson's Lancelot, Dostoyevsky's Raskolnikov, Joyce's Bloom, Melville's Billy Budd. Their names, as well as their personalities, make them memorable.

American Indians had an ear for names. An Apache warrior with a name like Geronimo had to be heroic, and how could a man named Cochise or Sitting Bull be ordinary?

In the early nineteenth century, Isabella, a canny freed slave, gave herself a name she did not intend for anyone to forget. They haven't. Sojourner Truth: Sojourner because she wandered from place to place speaking against slavery to anyone who would listen, and Truth because that is what she told.

The sixties produced a generation of children named Blueberry, Stormcloud and Maple. You probably haven't met them. Most of them have reinvented themselves as Bruce, Harold, and Susan. They have been voting Republican after finishing their MBAs at Wharton and Harvard.

Perhaps a writer has to be a poet like Sapphire to find a name for a character that evokes the irony and poignancy of Precious Jones—a black street girl, sixteen years old and pregnant, again, with her father's child—the first-person narrator of a novel called *Push*.

Before novelist Michael Dorris married Louise Erdrich, he adopted a three-year-old Lakota boy with severe disabilities, both physical and learning. Here is what he said about choosing a name for his son:

> I opened my mind, and there, like a time capsule that had waited for the most appropriate moment, was the symbol—because that's what names are, after all—that for me conveyed purity of soul, goodness, the perfection of creation: Abel. I later learned that in Hebrew, Abel means breath.

Save a page in your notebook just for names; they can sometimes inspire a story. For years I've wanted to find a story for twins I'll call Paris and Peter. I like to say Flaubert. Maybe a Bouvier de Flanders? One with a lot of class.

The names in the following suggestions for major and minor characters can and should be changed to fit your vision.

STORY STARTERS

☞ John had given your character the rottweiler she took everywhere. Mark told her they would get married when she got rid of the dog.

☞ A wealthy Chicago woman had many homes and many servants, but she was especially fond of her Polish housekeeper who had no friends or family in Chicago. She bought the housekeeper a talking bird to keep her company while her mistress was away. The plan worked too well. The housekeeper became obsessed with the bird—and only communicated by having the bird ask and answer questions, like "Cheeky, tell Mrs. Harper dinner is served."

☞ Your character rode the rodeo. She had been going down the road all her life. Her dad rode bulls; her mother broncos. Wildfire, her roping pony, was as famous as she. Then one day he broke his leg. Her father handed her the rifle. She could do it, or he would have to.

☞ Your character lived on the street, ate out of Dumpsters, but she bought milk for the cat who rode at the front of her cart, swiped from a supermarket. She thought the cat looked like the masthead on a ship. Then someone called the Humane Society.

☞ Your character has many problems with her family, her former husband, her colleagues at work, but she has no friends to talk to, only her goldfish, which is black. Write a monologue she delivers to her aquatic audience of one.

☞ Your character knew sometime she had to face her mother's being unable to continue living alone. Until she retired, her mother had taught English literature at a prestigious university, and had published a slim volume of lovely, lyrical poems. When your character flew out to visit her, her mother served her kibble and bits for dinner, but gave the cat fresh salmon. She said kitty was more reliable.

☞ Your character was a cop, a tough cop. Then he was transferred to the canine patrol.

☞ For five years, your character had worked with and admired Sybil, whose life seemed so calm and fulfilled. She spoke about the weekend excursions she and Spencer took, how she talked things over with him, told humorous stories about his rejecting some of her cooking failures. When your character's marriage failed, she had thought about suggesting an outing with Sybil, but assumed she would be busy with Spencer. It was only when Sybil didn't come to work and didn't call that she got her address from personnel and went to check on her. The super let your character in to the apartment. Sybil was dead. Spencer was a big tiger cat.

☞ Your character worked in an animal shelter, only because she couldn't find another job. She had never had a pet and didn't want one, but these creatures had such diverse personalities, she couldn't help but notice. Slowly one began to demand her attention. . . .

☞ Your character was the only female jockey at the track. She knew if she could ride Sun Dance, she could make a name for both of them.

☞ Your character's son had a dog he loved more than his family. The dog disappeared.

☞ Your character had owned Satan, a Doberman, for five years when he turned mean.

☞ Your character's parents ran a riding and boarding stable. There was a guy with glorious red hair who boarded a horse. Both were beautiful and hard to handle.

☞ Your character found her dream house on the outskirts of a picturesque village in Vermont. The realtor neglected to tell her the nearest neighbor—just down the road—raised billy goats and made Roquefort cheese to sell at a road-side stand.

☞ Your character's husband took their life savings to buy a herd of ostrich. All he had to do was convince people to eat the enormous eggs and to realize the meat was more tender and less fatty than beef. She thought of suing the awkward birds for alienation of affection.

☞ They met at a terribly fancy dog show. Your character was a judge. She was showing the ugliest Afghan he had ever seen.

☞ Your character went to a dude ranch for her one and only vacation of the year. Her horse ran away with her clinging to the saddle horn.

☞ Your character's mother called to tell him she was leaving her sizable fortune to her French poodle. Your character hated his mother and French poodles, but he loved money.

☞ Your character—a bachelor—had a pit bull. His next-door neighbor, a single mother, had a small daughter.

☞ He was a naturalist. Your character was a model. She didn't even know what an osprey was, but she went out on a boat with him to look for them. The boat left at four A.M.

The wind chapped her face and lips. Her head scarf blew away. Her jacket was soaked, and she had only worn one pair of thin socks.

☞ Your character's horse won the Triple Crown.

☞ Your character's wife accidentally backed over his dog, which was lying behind the back wheel.

☞ Your character's grandmother kept running away from the nursing home until he bought her a lazy lapdog. Be sure to develop the personality of the shiftless dog. I assume he would be chubby and have exotic tastes for something like chocolate-covered cherries.

☞ Your characters, a city couple with a shaky marriage, buy a summerhouse on the shore. They watch a raccoon with big soulful eyes and deft fingers rob their garbage can at night. The man wants to shoot him, but the woman calls the man a monster. They close up for the winter, leave everything neat and tidy. When they return the following summer, the rapacious raccoon has not only wrecked the place, but is now raising a family of marauders in the fireplace chimney. The man wants to build a roaring fire.

☞ When your character moved into the mountain cabin alone, she put out a salt lick near the stream. The first day a buck with a huge rack appeared. After a while, she would see two doe. Eventually, including the fawns, as many as eleven came in the early morning. The herd began to seem like the family she had chosen to leave. Then a hunter moved in on her side of the ridge.

☞ The trouble began when your character fell in love with the beauty and the brutality of the leopard.

CHAPTER 8

Objects to Start a Story

My paternal grandmother died before I was born, but in photos she looks like a combination of Gertrude Stein and Queen Victoria. She never smiled in pictures. Mother told me my father could not remember her ever having hugged him. My father said I got my expensive taste from her. When she died, she left a hundred-piece set of Havalin china. She had raised four children, but not even a cup handle had been chipped or broken. My aunt inherited the dishes. I remember a Thanksgiving dinner when we were served on Grandmother's china. I was five and a tomboy. I remember my mother looked as if she were praying all through the meal. When my aunt, who had no children, died, all one hundred pieces were still intact. Because I had my grandmother's taste, my aunt left the dishes to me. I gave them to a cousin. I told her the dainty pink flowers didn't fit my decor. If my grandmother had hugged my father, I would have changed the decor.

I can still visualize those delicate cups you could see

through if you held them to the light. What I've always seen was a story, but this is as much of it as I will ever tell.

When the motherless Brontë children were living in a parsonage on the lonely English moors in Yorkshire, their father, on a trip to Leeds, bought his only son, Branwell, a box of twelve wooden soldiers. Charlotte—the pushy one— grabbed the prettiest officer. She said he would be the Duke of Wellington. Emily chose a grave-looking fellow. After Anne and Branwell picked theirs, the siblings not only played war with the toys, but wrote its history waged in mythical lands, and created biographies for their soldiers.

In 1845 Emily and Charlotte published a volume of their poetry. Later Charlotte would admit only Emily's deserved publication. Only two copies sold but, undaunted, the sisters continued to work on their novels. *Wuthering Heights* and *Jane Eyre* were published in 1847. Emily's story of Heathcliff and Cathy's doomed passion shocked the Victorians, but has fascinated critics and readers ever since. For a long time there was a mystery surrounding the intense love story.

When Emily died at thirty, she had probably never been kissed. Charlotte is alleged to have believed her sister would not have perished if modesty had not prohibited her from allowing a doctor to examine her body. So where had the fire and fervor for Cathy and Heathcliff's love scenes come from? Early speculation whispered at the possibility of incest in the novel and in the home. Her talented but flawed brother Branwell was the only man Emily had ever known. Absolutely no evidence for that theory could be found outside of critics' imaginations, however.

When I was a graduate student, scholars had rediscovered Emily's poetry—many of the themes portrayed passionate love—and researchers were frantically seeking her unknown lover. Finally, someone remembered the toy soldiers and the children's early writing. Most everyone now concurs that the inspiration for the love poems and Heathcliff was Emily's grave little soldier, whom only someone without her imagination would see as wooden.

Jewelry rouses the muse for many writers. Guy de Maupassant found a source for painful irony in his short story "The Necklace," which turned out to have been paste. At a time when Fitzgerald found the rich fascinating, he wrote "The Diamond as Big as the Ritz." In school most of us were required to read John Steinbeck's *The Pearl*. The short parable about a Mexican fisherman, who finds a great pearl that brings evil to his family, was supposed to teach us a lesson.

Years ago I did my master's thesis on Henry James's *The Golden Bowl*. I could have done without the main lesson I learned. I hold a grudge. The central symbol of the story of illicit love is an exquisite, gilded crystal bowl that looks perfect until one holds it to the light, which reveals a crack. When the story opens Maggie, an inordinately rich, young American girl, is married to and madly in love with an Italian prince. He wants to buy the flawed bowl. She refuses because even though it doesn't show, she would know it was damaged. At the end, Maggie has learned the prince was lover to another woman, Charlotte, at the time Maggie married him, and he was still her lover when, later, Charlotte had become the young wife of Maggie's father.

I'm still angry at James, not because my thesis was so difficult to write, but for two significant reasons. First, I've never been able to create a symbol that even begins to have the impact of his bloody bowl, and when I try, the memory of his intimidates me. Most important, the story made such a powerful impression on my psyche no matter what the situation, I cannot forgive infidelity, which his novel convinced me to call betrayal.

SYMBOLS

Actually, James's antique bowl, a piece of cut crystal covered with gold leaf, had significance itself, but he brought a range of meanings to the object beyond its original intent. In reality a wedding ring is simply a circle of gold, but when a person flings it out the window of a moving car, as one of my cousins did, or buries it in the desert, as did a character in a story I once read, she is getting rid of more than a piece of jewelry.

Linus's security blanket ranks high in the importance of symbols in popular culture. Most of us have one. Mine, an old blue robe, has cloned itself. I have one at my sister's, another in a closet at my house on Bailey Island, two in

New York. Probably I wouldn't have become a writer if I could have found a job where I didn't have to wear shoes and panty hose. In the early days of my writing career, when I thought I'd probably starve, I bribed myself to keep trying by working barefooted, wearing my robe. Now I can't write a single word wearing clothes. Honest.

Clothes can become symbols. Try to imagine John Wayne in a black cowboy hat. A woman who wears a red wedding dress has a message. If a guy who doesn't work on Wall Street wears red suspenders, he is probably having an identity crisis. Teenagers with rips in their jeans would be horrified if you interpreted it as a poverty statement.

Writers use weather, as well as objects, symbolically. In Hardy's *The Return of the Native* if it hadn't been the hottest day of the year, Clym's mother wouldn't have died and his and Eustacia's problems might not have boiled over. Shakespeare's blowing and raging winds suggest what King Lear calls "the tempest of my mind." In Hemingway's *A Farewell to Arms,* after Catherine dies, Henry "left the hospital and walked back to the hotel in the rain."

Writers often create symbols unaware. If you're writing a story and something like a shooter marble continues to reappear in your adult character's pocket, it probably has more significance than you originally thought, but don't try to force gravity on something that can't support it. It could just be a marble. Symbols should grow naturally out of your material. Many fine stories have been written with no symbolic black clouds or regenerating sunrises.

Look in your jewelry box, kitchen cabinets, closet, fishing tackle box, desk drawer. If you don't see an object with a story, try one of the following:

STORY STARTERS

☞ Under a drawer liner, your character finds a letter, yellowed with age.

☞ When your character was six, his father gave him a red Flyer wagon. He rode kneeling on one knee in the bed, the other pushing, until he was flying away from his parents' angry voices. Today he buys only red cars.

☞   Your character's wife gives his old baggy sport jacket to the Salvation Army. She has no idea what a significant part of his history she has tossed away.

☞   Your character collected China bulls. She had a long shelf filled with every variety from Brahmas to Holsteins. Your story revolves around where and how she found some of them, and what lay behind her obsession.

☞   Your character remembers the wind chimes stirred melodically in the wind, allegro in a storm. In the spring there was always a storm.

☞   A sterling silver inkwell with a hallmark sat on your character's desk, always highly polished. It had been his father's. The inkwell was a reminder of what she had vowed/promised never to forget.

☞   Friends had chided your character about her cell phone, bought primarily for status. Then one day on the street she saw something dreadful. She was the one who called 911.

☞   Your character ran up some debts. What she took to the pawn shop had been his mother's. She lost the claim check.

☞   Your character had a lucky piece. He'd had a tad too much to drink when he gave it to the girl in the bar. Bad things began to happen.

☞   Your character always wore an antique cameo brooch, even on a T-shirt. The pin had a history.

☞   Your character kept the secret in his toolbox.

☞   He read your character's diary.

☞   He kept a picture of his first wife, who had died, in a silver frame on his chest of drawers. Your character was his second wife.

☞   Your character had a friend in the park. She needed one. She told him all her secrets. The roly-poly pig had been sculpted to tempt children to climb on his back, but an adult could find a cozy seat if no one was watching. The story opens at a time when no one was looking.

☞   Your character broke his mother-in-law's wedding present. He swore to her and to his wife that it was an accident, but secretly he enjoyed breaking things.

☞   Your character knew she was sorry she had married him.

Why else, after he had finished reading it, would she iron the newspaper before she would even glance at the ads.

☞   She saw the expensive statue of a chubby child in an antique store. It became an obsession.

☞   She wrote with a fountain pen and filled it only with purple ink.

☞   She touched his baby shoes she'd had bronzed, as she left the house to bail him out of jail again.

☞   Your character found a trunk in the attic.

☞   A lanky Italian security guard approached your character, looked her straight in the eye, and handed her a small glass charm with a tiny rosebud pressed inside. Realizing he would never see her again, he had said, "This is forever."

☞   All week your character looked forward to having lunch in the neighborhood restaurant after church. Alfred always seated your character at the table by the front window. Then one day a heavy-set man with Ben Franklin–type glasses and a wide gold watch chain stretched across his vest was sitting at her table.

☞   On a shelf in her closet, your character kept a lace-edged peach chiffon gown and negligee wrapped carefully in tissue. The box was from a pricey Fifth Avenue shop. Neither item had ever been worn.

☞   Your character found the letters tied with a blue ribbon in her bottom desk drawer.

☞   Your character always wore the watch, much too large for her narrow wrist. It had been her father's.

☞   Your character hated the grandfather clock. At night the chimes sounded gruff, as if it had a frog in its throat.

☞   Your character and his sister had been estranged for years. Then his mother died and left the contents of the house to them jointly. The lawyer had arranged for them to meet at the house on Saturday at ten A.M. All your character wanted was his father's revolver.

☞   Each ornament on your character's Christmas tree had special significance, but the glass angel for the top was the one she loved best. Tempted as she often was, she didn't allow herself to look at it until Christmas Eve, her ritualistic time to decorate the tree. This year her hands were shaking and she dropped it.

☞ Your character raised cacti. Not the flowering kind, but the variety with spiky needles.

☞ When your character lost the stone from her engagement ring, she took it as a sign.

☞ When he gave your character a cookie jar shaped like a pig, she took it personally.

☞ Just to hear a sound, your character often set the metronome to beating fast time.

☞ Your character slept with a thirty-year-old teddy bear.

☞ From the moment your character left the house, he wore his wedding ring in his watch pocket.

☞ Your character's uniform made him feel taller.

☞ Your character slept alone in a slinky black silk gown.

☞ Your character found it tucked between the cushions on the sofa. It changed her life.

☞ When your character moved to the city, she brought her saddle. It hung on the wall in her studio apartment.

☞ Your character rode his bicycle to his law firm, brought it up in the elevator, and propped it against the credenza in his elegant office. His partners did not approve.

☞ Wherever your character went, she collected hats of all shapes and sizes. She hated her hair. When she began wearing to bed a snood encrusted with dozens of sharp stones, her husband said it had gone far enough.

☞ Your character loved her ruby ring. It reminded her of blood. She liked the sight of blood.

☞ Your character's mother discovers at college her only son wears his Star of David under his T-shirt and he didn't even take a yarmulke.

☞ All your character had from her past was the quilt she had been wrapped in when she was left at the church. The quilt blocks had been made from material that looked new, perhaps scraps from sewing. The quilt eventually led her to the mother who had abandoned her.

CHAPTER 9

Settings to Start a Story

There's more to setting than geographic location.

My grandmother, who never hugged my father, built a beautiful Victorian home on her farm, or at least that's how it looked from the road. She had been dead and the house had been rented for a long time when it was first pointed out to me. "What was it like?" I asked my mother who had lived there during the first two years of her marriage. "Cold," she said. At least on a conscious level, I think Mother had meant "hard to heat."

The house had an ornate porch wrapped around the parlor sides like frothy frostening on half a cake. On the unadorned side, there was a practical back stoop leading to the kitchen, pantries, and mud room. Only company used the front door, my mother said.

Most farms have outbuildings scattered around at random. My grandmother's—standing in a straight row like solderers at inspection—didn't get out of line. As stark white as the house, they were all built from the same model but graduated in size from the big barn down to the small milk house. The scene, impressive and orderly, told a great deal about the person who had planned and maintained the property. It looked like the tidy place in which a woman who didn't smile in pictures or hug her kids would live.

Put your characters in places that reflect or affect their personalities. To discover if he is what he appears to be, put your sailing captain in a storm. Setting affects plot and character. People in Alaska don't think or behave like people who live in the tropics. Characters who have to be in control don't toss their soiled lingerie on the floor. They have a hamper.

For humor take your characters out of their element. Try to imagine one of the characters from the Broadway musical *Rent* at a ball with Henry Higgins. The producers of the television sitcom "The Beverly Hillbillies" kept this show going on one gag for years. The same premise explains the popularity of "Third Rock from the Sun," and "Alf" and "Mork and Mindy" before it. Perhaps the televisions staff borrowed their idea from Jonathan Swift, who wrote *Gulliver's Travels* in 1726.

Setting reflects the physical, and sometimes spiritual, background for the action of your story, as well as the time, period, and season of the year.

In her memoir *Under the Tuscan Sun,* Frances Mayes says one of the things she likes about Italy is that it's the only place in the world where she had ever taken a nap at nine in the morning. Have one your characters take a morning nap in Detroit, Chicago, Kansas City, St. Louis, Indianapolis, and prepare him to be struck by lightning.

Privileged Chinese women used to have their feet bound. Victorian women laced themselves into staves and didn't own a pair of jeans. Arab women cover their faces. Generation X women wear lace slips on the outside. You will have to decide how the clothes and the customs, reflecting the time or place, affect your character's sex lives.

Remember *Where I'm Calling From,* is the title of Raymond Carver's last collection of short stories. Always the good teacher, he left future writers a message.

TIME AND PLACE

As we touched on briefly in Chapter 1, telling the reader where and when your your story takes place is essential!

Ernest Hemingway once said he wanted to write so that you knew on every page what time it was and where the characters were. The setting can be Toledo, Ohio; Toledo, Spain; or a little town that exists only in your imagination, as long as you let your audience know where you and your characters are. Your tale can take place long ago and far away in a place that might have been. Just make it clear where you (the storyteller) are calling from.

There is no need to stop the action to say something as pedestrian as: "The setting for this story is June 1997, in Memphis Tennessee." You could say, "Actually, Elvis had been dead for years, but even today the Memphis merchants kept his spirit alive. It was good for business to make tourists believe they might see his gold Cadillac flash by at any minute."

Unless you plan to write a hundred thousand pages you never hope to publish, you will not be able to cover your character's entire life. The actual action can take place in one day, one week, one year, or ten, but you must make that decision before you begin to write and indicate when and how much time is passing.

Moving characters around in time and place can be clunky if you explain every action: "John was so angry at his wife he slammed the bedroom door and walked hurriedly down the hall to the steps that led to the front hall. He opened the door, stomped down the walk, turned right at the corner of Elm and Oak, and kept walking along the street until he reached the beach." You might say: "John had been so angry when he slammed out of their bedroom, he had walked a long way on the beach before he realized he was only wearing a T-shirt—no shoes, no socks, and ohmigod—no pants."

If the important part of your story takes place after the incident on the beach, you could say: "Ten years later in Paris, John could still remember how the cold wind had felt on his private parts, but the face of his former wife was vague. He hadn't seen her since the divorce." If the story focuses on that one crucial day, the next line could be: "In a few minutes, Ellen found John huddled behind a large piece of driftwood. She threw the beach towel over his head. Worst of all, she laughed."

Writers like Edgar Allan Poe and Kafka, however, have

written stories that never move out of their narrators' warped imaginations. Their thoughts create the weirdest landscapes of all.

Sam Shepard was teasing when he chose *Cruising Paradise* as the title for his short stories. A boy travels to a desolate roadside inn to retrieve the charred mattress on which his drunken father burned to death; a couple quarrel desperately and part in a South Dakota motel room; in Los Angeles a woman thinks she cutting through a watermelon rind, but it's her husband's little finger.

Zia Faffrey's *The Invincible: A Tale of the Eunuchs of India* is a nonfiction account based on research and interviews with real people, but think what a unique idea for a novel she has uncovered. Within the folds of India, she found a secret world descended from the days of palaces and harems that survives in ghostly form. At least a half million eunuchs, a shadowy subculture echoing cruel and ancient sexual practices, still sing and dance at births and weddings and act as male prostitutes. Rumors suggest eunuchs kidnap young males to replenish their numbers and disabled boys are donated to the eunuch societies. It's a plot for a social reformer like Dickens.

If exotic settings appeal to you, the nomads in India who travel with camels and sheep offer another wondrous adventure for your characters.

Cormac McCarthy has chosen the rugged border country between Mexico (the old) and the United States (the new) not only as a literal setting for his stories, but as a rite of passage for his characters. In *The Crossing,* Billy Parham sets off on a quest that leads him not only across the border, but from adolescence to adulthood.

Writers have built their reputations on settings. John Steinbeck said he couldn't afford a ticket when Fitzgerald, Hemingway, Ford Madox Ford, and his peers were going to Paris. He stayed at home in California and wrote about the lives of people in Monterey and the Salinas Valley—or people like the Joads in *The Grapes of Wrath* who end up there. His settings for *Tortilla Flat, The Red Pony, The Wayward Bus, Of Mice and Men* are mainly rural areas where people live close to the land and where malevolent natural forces like drought can be as destructive as human greed.

When I travel, I like to read regional novels for the local
color of the places I'm visiting. The first time I saw the
rocky coast of Maine, it didn't take my breath away, it stole
my heart. When we used to go for a week's vacation I cried
most of the time we were there—because we would have
to leave. The Bar Harbor Library had a small closetlike
room reserved for novels set in Maine. I remember my disappointment the day the librarian told me she was sorry,
but I had read every one she had to offer. At that time,
one still signed the card. I checked. She was right. I don't
remember the characters or the plots in those stories, but
I remember the storms, the fog, the doughnuts (there were
always storms and fog and doughnuts), the gulls, the salt
ponds, the smell of the briny air, the lobster boats, but
mainly the sea. I own a house on Bailey Island now. The
realtor should have split her commission with Sarah Orne
Jewett and Ruth Moore.

My house sits in about eight or nine inches of soil on a
rocky point. The next parish is Ireland. Every year an angry
sea reaches up and gulps someone off the granite ledge.
Last year a moose came to my back door. When we tried
and he allowed a friend and me to pet his nose, the author-
ities they took the moose away by helicopter to wherever
strange animals go. They've allowed me to stay, but the
locals look at me funny or tell horrifying stories about people who have been killed hideously by moose, which are
not household pets. The moose wouldn't have scared my
father. What would have horrified him was my using hard-
earned money to buy land that wouldn't grow a thing but
beach roses with prickly thorns.

I call my house on Bailey Island, "Point of View." Many
people—especially writers—name cars, boats, houses.
Camelot may or may not have been King Arthur's kingdom,
but Jackie Kennedy convinced the world Camelot existed
once again—just for a little while—on Pennsylvania Avenue. Recently, I read a story about a cottage on a lake that
had served as refuge for a large family for a long time. They
had come to call it Wegona because every summer the aunt
and uncle who owned it would say, "We're gonna add a
deck or more bedrooms or a larger kitchen. . . ."

If you have read Daphne du Maurier's *Rebecca*, you
might not remember the plot, but I would bet you remem-

ber Manderley. I once went to Cornwall just to see that house . . . you can't. It was still there, but so are the iron gates, and it hides behind a thick woods. On that trip I didn't see any pirates in Penzance either, but on the way down I did walk across Hardy's Heath. The wild ponies who used to surround Diggory Venn's wagon still roam.

Wuthering Heights, Bleak House, Tara, those houses, as real as the characters who inhabited them, were created by what Laurie Colwin used to call "domestic sensualists." The authors found the inspiration to make a picture appear made out of language like ". . . the bloody glory of the sunset colored the fresh-cut furrows of Georgia clay to even redder hues. . . . The whitewashed brick plantation house seemed an island set in a wild red sea. . . ." Giving those places names was like passing out calling cards. The gates to Manderley were locked, so I closed my eyes and remembered ". . . Manderly, secretive and silent . . . the grey stone shining in the moonlight . . . The terrace sloped to the lawns, and the lawns stretched to the sea. . . ."

After the painful divorce ending a long marriage, Frances Mayes and her second husband wanted a fresh start in their own place. They fell in love with a house in Tuscany appropriately called "Bramasole," "from *bramare,* to yearn for, and *sole,* sun."

Anne Tyler's Homesick Restaurant served as the novel's metaphor as well as giving it a title. You can have fun inventing names for places where your characters hang out. As long as you don't get carried away, a light sprinkle of puns can be fun, like a coffee shop called Sufficient Grounds, a beauty shop known as Shear Madness. Clip Joint could be a barbershop, or maybe a pub.

You can make up names for towns like Carolyn Chute's Egypt, Maine, or Li'l Abner's Dogpatch, but it's hard to improve on the inspiration of some founding fathers. My sister has just moved to Romeo; that's in Michigan, just down the road from a big Ford plant, not owned or operated by either the Montagues or the Capulets.

Sandburg's image of Chicago, "Hog Butcher to the World," lasted longer than the stockyards. When I read Thomas Mann's *The Magic Mountain,* I couldn't help but wish I had tuberculosis. The first time I saw the ancient walls surrounding the colleges at Oxford, I kicked one. It hurt my toe, but I did it for Jude (the obscure), the stone mason they wouldn't let into the hallowed academic halls.

Most of us have nostalgic sentiments, sweet as chocolate pudding, about some special place, but for a "not what you expect" twist, don't forget those places we abhor, like funeral homes, hospitals, and divorce courts. Two of the worst hours of my life were spent in the basement of funeral parlors choosing caskets for my father and father-in-law, talking to undertakers who must learn that guilt-laced language in a course called "How to Make a Bloody Fortune out of Bereavement." Never again, I vowed. My mother and I agreed we should all know better than ever to write a big check to anyone who utters a euphemism like bereavement. We joked about the ersatz sympathy, the used-car salesman's language. The only time I smiled for a long time after my mother died was the day the mortician said, " 'Mom' wouldn't want you to skimp on what she'll rest in for eternity. She'd want to be comfortable." My sister was horrified when I said, "No, my *mother* would rather my sister and I took tap-dancing lessons with the money we're about to spend on this monstrosity."

Before you begin to write, close your eyes. Visualize the place where your story occurs. Turn your pen or computer into a camera. When your character fits herself into the enormous leather recliner, her father's chair, how does it feel on her bare legs? Does she expect the chair to throw her like a one-rider horse? Or does she feel she's earned the right to the throne? Is the chair in a study on Park Avenue, a family room in Peoria, a Mews house in London? Does it matter? Is she sitting there today or in a memory of when she was ten?

STORY STARTERS

☞ The content of Milton's refrigerator/medicine cabinet told the story.

☞ Your character arrives at college to find his roommate from Bangladesh has already moved in and decorated his side of the room.

☞ The locals said the original owner of the house refused to leave, no matter who held the deed. After your character bought the place, at night she often heard strange sounds that couldn't be explained.

☞ Your character moved into the barn. He was more comfortable there than in the house where he didn't feel wanted.

☞ It began as their dream house and turned into an ongoing nightmare when your character became so obsessed with the house that it meant more to her than her family or friends.

☞ Your character's father dies, and your character goes back to clean out his dad's law office. The story takes place in one day in the office, where your character finally comes to know his enigmatic father.

☞ Your character, a great admirer of John Kennedy, joins the Peace Corps when she retires from teaching at age sixty-five. She is sent to . . .

☞ Your character had spent years of his life, racked up monumental student loans, training to be a surgeon. When he finally finishes his residency and finds a job in a hospital, the atmosphere is sinister. The staff make him think the loonies have taken over the asylum.

☞ Your character fell in love with a commercial airline pilot. He was based in Los Angeles. She lived in Chicago. She was already engaged to him before she saw where he lived. His apartment told her things she did not want to know about the man she had agreed to spend the rest of her life with.

☞ Your character had discovered the bar his first week in the new city eight years ago. It was more home than his apartment around the corner, the regulars more like family than the people he dutifully visited once each year. Then one night, after too much to drink, he ruined everything.

☞ Your character, a socialite and noted philanthropist, had married well after coming East to college. Her sister had married the boy from a nearby farm back home in Iowa. Their car was hit by a train. The sister and her husband were both killed. Your character was her niece's guardian.

☞ Your character, a reporter for a large city newspaper, receives an assignment to cover an arranged wedding between a fourteen-year-old girl from a nomadic Pakistani tribe and a forty-five-year-old widower who has many camels and many children. The wedding will take place at an oasis in the desert.

☞ Covering the . . . war, your character, a foreign correspondent, falls in love with someone from the other side.

☞ Your character is asked to house-sit for someone who will be in Europe for six months. It changes her life.

☞ Your character, a hardworking blue-collar bloke, buys a raffle ticket from a kid. He wins a month-long cruise on a luxury liner. He buys a tuxedo, a pair of white flannels, a blue blazer, and sails away.

☞ Your character rents a small garden plot in a vacant lot that becomes the dominant metaphor in your story.

☞ In a desk drawer, your character finds a single sheet of engraved stationery from Neverbe, the house he has tried so unsuccessfully to forget.

☞ Your character's studio was his life. He lived there in that perfect light with his muse. He found the eviction notice in the freight elevator. The building had been bought by a developer. He had thirty days.

☞ Your character's father has lobstered off the island for as long as she can remember. When he dies and she plans to continue to run his traps, the other fishermen are not prepared to welcome a woman. Not all of the obstacles they put in her way are subtle.

☞ Your character inherited five hundred acres of rich farmland in Kansas.

☞ It had started out as a squat, but your character and a child, who had been abandoned like the building, turned it into a home.

☞ Your character left a note: "I've had it. Don't try to find me." He went to Ireland, rented a tinker's wagon, and kept on the move.

☞ Your character tried out for the ballet corps and was accepted at sixteen. It was not only her toes that had to develop calluses.

☞ Your character went to the island for a week's vacation. He just never went home.

☞ They had become friends when their husbands were partners at a prestigious law firm. Your character is still married, but her friend has been divorced for five years and has moved back to St. Louis where she came from. On a business trip, your character calls her old friend

☞ Your character is a career sailor. She is hired to deliver boats all over the world. The storm happens when she agrees to return home a Danish boat that has competed in the big cup race in Boston.

☞ Your character marries a Native American jewelry maker she meets at a craft show. They go back to live on the reservation.

☞ Something magical happens to your character on a ski slope.

☞ Your story takes place on Christmas Eve, which was neither a silent nor holy night when your character's family came home for the holidays.

☞ Your character, an engineer, hired her out of the union hall. All he needed was a backhoe operator, not trouble on the job.

☞ Your character began living at the mall after she had an argument with her mother over a tank top her mother wouldn't let her buy. That was a year ago. Her biggest problem was when they changed security guards.

☞ Your character joined a rock band. They lived in a hallucinated state on a converted bus that also took them from gig to gig.

☞ Your character passed the interview with the board of an exclusive cooperative apartment. Only after she moved in did she begin to feel the hostility. She didn't always receive her mail. Packages and deliveries were not always accepted. She even felt as if the handyman might purposely have broken her VCR. After a while, other tenants began to behave strangely when she got on the elevator. She suspected the super of foul play.

☞ Your character lived on a houseboat in San Francisco Bay. She was asleep when the storm began. When she woke up she was drifting under the Golden Gate Bridge.

CHAPTER 10

Sports

After a few tumbles, we all learn to walk. Most of us can ride a bike without training wheels. Only the few can slam dunk, run faster than a gazelle, knock one out of the park, connect a pass, dance on her toes, make a hole in one, hit a bull's-eye, ride a bull, break a bronco, put a shot, jump the high hurdles, dance and twirl on ice, return a fast serve, swim the butterfly stroke, pole vault. Those who can and do, or those who try but fail, fascinate us on the playing fields or on the page.

Here's the challenge for you. The demand for good sports stories exceeds the supply. In most categories from mysteries and romance to belles lettres, publishers receive more manuscripts than they can find space to stack them. And lawyer stories? They have a few. But there are not enough novels like *The Natural, The Loneliness of the Long-Distance Runner,* and *Shoeless Joe.*

My theory and a token will take you to Brooklyn, but I believe this deficiency explains one of the reasons the

United States does not have the number of readers we would like. Anyone who teaches younger children knows boys wear out copies of *The Contender, Moves Make the Man,* and *Hoops,* the biographies of heroes like Joe Louis, Michael Jordan, Chris Evert, Babe Ruth, but when they run out of stories about athletes, the majority tend to move outside to bat the ball around, hang out in the gym with the coach. Those who "have it" soon spend their free time at practice. At home, too many of those who have it, and those who don't but wish they did, go into training to loll on the couch with dad watching golf, football, tennis, basketball, on the telly.

Your learn to write by writing! Most often those who understand how it feels to strengthen a muscle, perfect their timing, go in for a layup, or tackle two hundred pounds of solid muscle, spend their formative years doing it, not finding the words to describe the sensation. That's your challenge. The first step: Delete the words and phrases used in office memos to cloak what's happening and who's doing what to whom, like "it has been decided," "action will be taken." The passive voice won't work in any story, but especially not in a sports story. You have to show who whacked/smacked/socked/smashed whom.

LANGUAGE TO FIT THE STORY

When Wislawa Szymborska, a Polish poet, won the Nobel Prize for Literature in 1996, she said after Poland lost six million people—nearly one-fifth of its population—in World War II, it was not possible to use the same language as before. The poets writing from "the margins of Europe" felt the need to use a very simple, very brash, vernacular. They wanted a poetry without artifice. Those who survived the war and the Holocaust could never use an elaborate, ornamental, or sonorous language again.

Words must not only communicate your message, but reflect the emotion, the mood, the tone, and even the beat of what you wish to convey. Today Polish poetry often offers an expiation, a hope for redemption that springs from their philosophical and ethical seriousness.

In my workshops, Andy wrote from the viewpoint of a drugged-out rock musician. The speedy speech was vulgar, repetitive, laced with jargon, idioms—the lingo of the world he portrayed. Barbara's story set in New York during the Victorian Age flows at the languid pace of the languorous lives ladies lived. Even the action—death by disease, murder, and betrayal—while gripping, does not gallop. The impact flows over you, lingering on the pain and suffering.

Subject dictates language. Look at the sports page. You find phrases recapitulating the color, the action, the drama, the excitement, the voracity of the players, the involvement of the writer. Players have to stick to the rules, but sports writers make up phrases like "chin music" and "slam dunk" that might not be grammatically correct, but paint the picture. Sports vernacular is loud, bombastic, vibrant, fast-paced. Recent headlines: "TOASTED: Eagles Grill Brown," "Rangers Demolish Canadiens," "Colts Kick Bills," "Paterson (Or Was It Jordan?) Sparkles," "Yanks Didn't Want to Choke on His Hefty Contract."

Think strong verbs with built-in sound tracks and a vivid image: smack, sock, swat, squash, squish, zap, zip, zonk, zoom.

Try to choose verbs to fit the character. A two-hundred-and-fifty-pound tackle doesn't meander around the field. Recently, I read an account of a con man who "hightailed" it to a gala in Egypt to pick pockets.

You won't have to search further than your own sensitivity to find the words for the emotional side of sports. Envy, rejection, defeat, unrequited love, and competition sound and feel the same if you hang your clothes in a locker, your bedroom closet, a star's dressing room, or on a nail on the wall.

The ability to play sports, or the lack of it, has created havoc in many families, and the potential for dozens of stories with built-in conflict.

In a community where sports were held in high regard, I was academic and my sister was athletic. If we had been male, I would probably be on Prozac. The town tried to make it a problem. Fortunately, we had an extremely wise mother. "Self-esteem" hadn't yet invaded the language, but Mother kept a hefty supply in the kitchen cabinets. The gods who like to joke around played a dirty trick on me.

They gave me a body that looked as if I should be a good athlete, but they forgot the coordination. The tennis dress fit, but put a racket in my hand and I looked like a gazelle. When I was a lifeguard and giving lessons, my little sister demonstrated the dives. I had the words to explain how to do it. She had the grace. I made the A's in English, and her teachers said to her, "But your sister knew where to put the commas, how to make it interesting." Mother said, "Both of my daughters are so talented. Lou can write stories, but Loann is the better dancer."

Down the street two brothers were not so lucky. One boy, captain of the football team—just what his father had ordered—had a younger brother who was small and who suffered from asthma and from his father's disappointment. Even today, I don't think the brothers send Christmas cards.

Aging comes slinking up on all of us and refuses to be shooed away by the plastic surgeon or the makeup artist, but the black-hooded betrayer spooks jocks more than most. As A. E. Housman said, athletic "glory does not stay." Fame has an addictive component as powerful as nicotine. Not all well-known athletes find a second career with as much exposure as politicians Bill Bradley or Jack Kemp. Tom Buchanan, a minor character in Fitzgerald's *The Great Gatsby,* had found life downhill after his heroic performance in the Yale-Princeton game. John Updike's basketball champ, Rabbit, ends up selling Toyotas. I think you can find a story in the image of the quarterback sitting in the empty stands after the cheering has stopped.

We can handle other people's problems with a stiff upper lip. The player injured in his prime or one who falls with a dread disease makes a gripping story, but don't overlook the humorous angle for a sports yarn.

My sister and I both married men, one 6'3", one 6'4", who were uncomfortable in hotel beds, theater seats, and airplane seats. Finding jackets and shirtsleeves to cover their wrists could be a challenge. My nephew, Dannon, came packaged with the same problems. Then for a few years he raced BMX bikes and developed thighs jean designers did not have in mind. When he began lifting weights, he couldn't buttons his shirt collars. These family concerns began to seem trivial, however, when Dannon landed a job on the management side of the Cleveland Cavaliers. One day when I was having lunch with him near the Gund Arena, one of the Cavs players walked past, slapped Dannon on the shoulder and said, "Yo, little man." Little man, indeed. I was incensed until my nephew said, "Auntie Lou, he's six-nine."

I haven't been able to get that guy out of my mind. His jacket was as long as my good black dress. And his shoes? A cat and a couple of kittens could have found a comfortable home in one of them. And what if he marries a woman 5'2" who weighs 110 pounds? Speaking clinically, the placement of our reproductive organs is sort of comical in the best of situations, but I would assume this man would have to be inventive in bed as well as under the basket. I'd wager you could find a publisher immediately for a well-written sports story that tickled his funny bone.

No matter what the subject matter, and especially in a sports story, try for "the not what you expect." Although touching and sometimes even tragic, the promising hoop player from the ghetto who blows his career through his nose has been told oh so many times. When I saw *Hoop Dreams* as a book review headline and thought the plotline would be yet another version of a Michael Jordan who could have but didn't make it, I almost ignored it. Fortunately, I didn't. Charley Rosen's novel, *The House of Moses All-Stars,* set in 1936, tells the adventures of six Jews and the Irish Catholic son of a New York cop, who make up a basketball team of rascals called the House of Moses All-Stars. The team members travel around the country in a hearse with a Star of David painted on the side, and take to the court wearing yarmulkes and long beards. Rosen might not win the next National Book Award, but you have to admire him for changing your perspective on the possibility for a story about guys in short pants who bounce a ball around.

Don't overlook the possibilities for plots in lesser-known sports. Fencing and polo attract aristocrats, and the clothes are so stylish and such fun to describe. Traditionally, the pool hall has served as a metaphor for the tough guy's hangout. You might try a "not what you expect" twist. I once had an editor whose husband stayed home to raise the kids. Their oldest daughter became a pool shark who traveled the circuit. Until Tonya Harding began to play dirty, the ice rink suggested grace and gentility. Ballroom dancers and gymnasts haven't had much exposure in literature. I would certainly read a story about the women who drive hackney ponies wearing silk dresses, panty hose, fancy hats. And there will never be enough rodeo stories to satiate my desire.

A popular sport story told from a different point of view could be fun, like a baseball tale as seen through the eyes of the bat boy or the umpire or the hot dog vendor or the coach for the other team.

Don't overlook women's sports. Dannon grew up in Iowa. Molly, his first serious girlfriend, knew how to dance cheek to cheek, but she also shot hoops and played poker with the guys. That year Dannon's team got beat out in the sectionals, but Molly's took the state women's basketball championship.

If you have a proclivity for tough types and language that sizzles, you might want to create a character who plays hockey. I wonder if the players who put on those uniforms, which make them look brutish before they make a move, feel when they're dressed like that, they have to be rowdy to live up to the image. Here's a hockey headline in the *Times*, known by the other papers in town to be the panty-waists of sports language: "Palffy and a Stingy Salo Keep Islanders Stoking." The article says he zigged and zagged his way to the zone. A rugged rookie got blown out. The hit left him stunned and sprawled. Someone else needed stitches to close a gash after a slap shot. Another spent the night in the hospital with a concussion.

Without spilling a drop of blood, you might be able to find a way to play the game with the following:

STORY STARTERS

☞ They both joined the ballet corps at fifteen, became partners right away. He was strong, but not handsome. She was delicate and lovely. When they became famous, everyone focused their cameras and their stories on her. When he finally admitted to himself how much he hated her, it began to affect their performance, and finally their personal lives.

☞ Three weeks before the Olympic tryouts, her swimming coach said casually, "Watch your weight. Appearance makes a difference." In two weeks she was bulimic. By the tryouts she had lost her strength.

☞ In college, she had led the cheering squad, been pledged by the best sorority, served as Homecoming Queen. After graduation, she married the captain of the basketball team, who was drafted by the NBA. Very soon, she found sitting in the stands, clapping with the other wives, wasn't what she'd had in mind.

☞ They worked the high wires without a net. Then one night he didn't catch her. Rumors persisted that he had motivation for missing.

☞ He was the family's hope. When he went down, he could hear, as well as feel, the bones in his knee shatter.

☞ She had been the star on the circuit for a long time. Then the crowds became fascinated by a youngster whose putt was poetic, they said.

☞ By the time their children were in elementary school, it was obvious Jane would be big, tall, homely, and athletic, but her brother would be slight, artistic, and beautiful. The family did not handle it well.

☞ This was an NBA team that had a good racial mix. The players got along on the court and off. Their wives socialized. The fans were supportive. Then the new, angry draftee came with a sullen, hateful attitude, and he played the race card.

☞ The guy grew up in terrible poverty. When he became a world-class athlete, no one could blame him when he endorsed everything from jockey shorts to jumping ropes. Tell the story from the time he has enough money to buy anything except privacy and freedom. He has become a prisoner who can no longer take a walk alone, stop in the pub for a beer, go to a movie without creating a riot.

☞ The story opens when the former champ—a little punch drunk—is parking cars in Vegas, hoping for a comeback. His right hook had been more impressive than his IQ scores, but he had been a good-hearted guy whose handlers flattered him and stole his money. When it is obvious he won't fight again, he goes after the handlers who have the new champ.

☞ Your character came to the city to be an actress, but ended up working in a sports bar. She became friends with the star hockey player who stopped in most nights. When he asked her to marry him, he told her he was gay but he needed a wife, he cared for her like a sister, he would give her a luxurious life and never embarrass her. She accepted.

☞ His bar is called The Huddle. The jersey he had worn ten years ago, the team pictures, the pennants, and some shots of him with celebrities hang on the wall. He'll tell anyone who will listen about the Super Bowl he played in. He still remembers how many people came to the parade, what the mayor said in his speech.

☞ She ran the sailing club, gave lessons to the kids, crewed in a race on the big boats when needed. A little beach house came with the job. She had never been happier. Then she and one of the club members fell in love. He was married, had two kids. His wife's father was on the club's board.

☞ Her father loved to play golf, but he was an average player. When she showed early promise of being outstanding, he pushed her like a stage-door mom. At eighteen she could no longer take the pressure, nor face her dad's heartbreak. One day she simply disappeared.

☞ She was the flight attendant on the plane chartered to bring the football champs home. The exuberant team got out of hand, spraying the cabin with champagne, throwing desserts at each other, tackling the attendants in the aisle. A couple of the guys asked your character to go out celebrating with them at the end of the trip. She adamantly refused. After the team had deplaned, she discovered one of them had taken with him her flight bag containing her clothes, makeup, and jewelry case. He had left a card with his address where she could pick it up.

☞ Your character had played for the team he had dreamed about, in the city he loved, for ten years. Then he got traded.

☞ He had begun gambling a little just to relax after the pressure of the season. Money wasn't a problem. He had a sweetheart of a contract. Then he began to lose big time. When he was in serious trouble, the casino owner offered him an out. It would only involve throwing one game.

☞ Even when the stalker wasn't around, she could feel his presence. Her coach thought she was being paranoid, even when the guy began to heckle her in the stands. When the shot hit her serving arm, she dropped her racket. Stunned, she watched the blood soak her favorite white shorts.

☞ She was at five thousand feet and on her way down the mountain when the storm hit. Ten minutes later she hit the ice. She knew nothing, not even a helicopter, could fly in weather like this.

☞ In an instant your character realized he had made a lousy call. He felt bad enough. Then in the parking lot, he found a group of thugs surrounding his car. One had a tire iron, another an empty whiskey bottle.

☞ They had skated together since they were kids, always competed as partners. He thought he might even love her. Then he had an outstanding offer that didn't include her.

☞ The other Little League parents began to avoid them. She didn't blame them. Her husband heckled, interfered, and pushed their son beyond the limit. But your character's husband intimidated her, too. Then the coach called to say either she talked her husband into backing off, or the boy couldn't play on any of the teams.

☞ His sexual preference had always been for men, but he had played the artful dodger through high school and college, always having a female date for big occasions. When he made the NFL, he met Randy, with whom he hoped to spend the rest of his life. Randy felt the same way, but he refused to have a clandestine relationship. Your character played for a team in a town that did not have a politically correct attitude toward homosexuals.

☞ Your character's older brother, their father's favorite, played for the other team. Their father was in the stands.

☞ In high school they were best buddies, played on the same team, knew each other's moves. Your character went to

West Point. His buddy went to the Naval Academy. Your story takes place the day of the Army-Navy game.

☞ She was good enough to play on the boys' team. Your character is the coach who has the dilemma of dealing with the flack—perhaps a lawsuit—if he doesn't allow her to suit up (and yes, to travel) and with the problems he anticipates with his team. Two of the guys are macho maniacs, and one has an extreme crush on the pretty girl who wants to play.

☞ His father rode to the hounds, his cousin played polo, his sister had taken ballet lessons since she was five. Your character wanted to wrestle. The family was horrified.

☞ The press loved your character on and off the gridiron. He was articulate, cooperative, would make school appearances. He had an attractive wife and cute kids who would put up with interviews for feature stories. He had simply gone for a routine physical when the blood sample showed he was HIV positive. Your story could deal with the lie he tells the public and his family, while the true story he reveals to the reader in interior monologues.

☞ Your character came to New York with a dream. He would dance on Broadway, become the new Gene Kelly, Tommy Tune. Your story finds him giving ballroom dancing lessons at Arthur Murray.

CHAPTER 11

Memories

Without even going to City Hall, writers receive a license to lie. What a relief not to have to try to remember how things really happened, but to be able to make situations worse, better, bigger, braver, more embarrassing, dramatic, sillier. Memories are always imperfect. J. Alfred Prufrock admits there is always "time yet for a hundred indecisions, and for a hundred visions and revisions."

Passion distorts reality. Love blows people and events into bold capital letters. Envy shrinks. Disappointment darkens. Regrets distort. Fear exaggerates.

Recently, Dannon read a dramatic incident I had recalled about him and a basketball coach who had put extraordinary pressure on him in a big game. "Part of it was true," my nephew, who has a generous nature, said. "I was a sophomore." I imagine the coach would say, "Whaaat's she talking about?" Point of view also distorts reality (see p 133).

Delving into your protagonist's memories offers one of the more effective means of revealing her character. If she remembers fifth grade, but had no best friend, you've aroused curiosity. If he clenches his fist as he talks about his first job, his first wife, his first child, we want to know why. If she says her adolescence had no bumps, I detect an unreliable narrator. If he says that, of course, my parents made mistakes, but they can't be held responsible for my behavior at thirty-five, I would accept an invitation to his family reunion.

The tone of your character's memories tells more than her actual subject. One of my students, Nina, who was born in Siberia, insists a translator cannot capture the heavy darkness, the bleakness, of Dostoyevsky's viewpoint. *Notes from the Underground* begins with this: "I am a sick man . . . I am a spiteful man. I am an unpleasant man. I think my liver is diseased." He goes on to say he would like to be an insect. His servant, an old woman, he tells us, is spiteful, stupid, and smells bad. Bleaker than the above would be hard to bear. As the narrator shares memories of his career as a low-level civil servant, he shows no respect for himself, his fellow man, and as his rantings continue, he reveals he doesn't have such a high regard for his reader either. He blames the system.

Imagine your character, an eighties Wall Street bond trader, remembering his financial ruin—the day one of his big issues, one he couldn't cover, was called. What tone would you have him take? Which of the following has the possibility for the most dramatic effect? "Greed was contagious and I caught a good case of it, but I've learned my lesson." "The system was out of control, and I was a victim. That stupid Reagan and his Beltway Boys didn't know a damn thing about economics." "My dad passed on his lousy values—make a buck as fast as you can, any way you can." "Hey man, I don't sweat it. Up today, down tomorrow. That's the game. It keeps the adrenaline pumping. As soon as the SEC raises the restriction, I'll be back. Just the other day I heard about this sweet deal. . . ."

What if your character recalls when she ran for president of her high school class, but lost? She could say (in a self-righteous tone) her high IQ defeated her because the other frivolous kids cared more about boys, basketball, and bosoms. Or she could say the same thing in an ironic—slightly self-deprecating—tone and the reader would like her because she had a sense of humor. They could also like the first approach, even if they didn't find the protagonist sympathetic, because they would feel superior to the narrator, who couldn't see her own faults the way the readers could. When setting up your story, and deciding what effect you want to have on your audience, don't overlook tone. Keep in mind, we might think we would like for our friends and lovers to be saints with sunny dispositions, but we like to read about characters whose flaws, quirks, and blind spots show just like ours.

Although memories present a plethora of material, structuring the story so the reader recognizes time and place must be done with care and caution. The action happened before your story opens. Presenting the narrator in the here and now, but moving back in time, comes with a challenge.

FLASHBACKS

In "Cats," John Updike's short story, the first line says, "When my mother died, I inherited eighty acres of Pennsylvania and forty cats." In a few sentences he describes his being in her house at the present time, preparing for her funeral. Notice the change in tense when he moves into memories about his mother. "She had been born here, in the age of mule-drawn plows. Neither my father nor I had understood her wish to return to this weary place of work. . . ."

The past perfect tense signals the reader to a switch in time and place—a flashback to what has gone before—or at least the way the narrator remembers what has gone before.

In addition to the change in tense, you must create a transition (a bridge) from present to past and back again to the present. Updike says, "In deference to my asthma she had never let the cats in the house, but the day after she died they could hear me. . . . I spoke to them much as she had."

Updike wrote his story in first person, making the experience more intimate, but you would use the same techniques if your narrator were telling the story in third person from your character's point of view: "Joe went back to the farm and the forty cats he inherited the day his mother died. . . . Neither Joe nor his father had understood why she wanted to move back. . . ."

Funerals, weddings, and reunions grant good opportuni-

ties to flashback to memories. Regrets trigger remem-
brances of mistakes, misunderstandings Your character
wishes he had told his father the truth before he died. She
regrets she had not been able to see Jerry's attributes before her cousin had married him on the rebound. He rues
the days he had let fickle Mary Lou Price wreck his concen-
tration on the field and in physics class.

Stories about childhood innocence, humiliations, disappointments—the universal experiences—touch us all. So
does unrequited puppy love, the first time, or the one your
character never got over. It is hard to write a bad story
about Daddy's girl or Mamma's boy.

Homesickness hurts worse than appendicitis. A young
child's lack of it could betray family secrets.

A river—not as famous as Norman MacLean's—ran
through our county creating rick bottomland that produced more grain per bushel—than when the land wasn't
flooded. I was probably eight or nine when I went to spend
a week with a friend thirty miles away. The river rose and
flooded the highway, making it impossible for me to go
home. Obviously, I didn't die as I expected every night
when I cried myself to sleep. Eventually, the friend's family
realized my dire condition. They drove me as far as they
could, and my father rescued me in a rowboat. If you think,
in our age, there aren't any heroes, you should have seen
my father appear out of the fog in that rowboat.

You probably have an attic full of memory symbols: your
scout badges, track medals, yarmulke from your bar mitz-
vah, regional math award, baseball cards—one with
Mickey Mantle's actual signature. Be generous. Dust them
off and give the stuff to your character. Include the blood,
sweat, and tears they're wrapped in. *Write from experience
not about it.* The story will be more interesting if your character thinks he will be sent to hell because his dad actually
tied the knots your character claimed he had tied for the
scouting badge. It's okay to use the material now. You're
writing fiction. Besides your scout master has probably retired and moved to Florida.

Recently, I ran across my wings. I'll never stand as tall
again as I did the day Pat Paterson, the chairman of United
Air Lines, pinned them on my uniform. That crisp navy blue
suit and cocky cap did more for my ego than any designer's

outfit ever has. For years I've tried unsuccessfully to weave some of those experiences into a novel. It's a crummy story. Bad things must have happened, but I can't find the conflict. My letters from those years usually begin with, "You won't believe what happened to me today. . . ." But from my view-point what had happened was always exciting, thrilling, in-credible. I seemed even to have loved what the airlines called "irregular operations," which meant we were fogged in in Philly for three days, the return trip was canceled, and the crew scheduled for a turnaround didn't get home from New York for days. When we blew a tire on landing in Omaha and I had to evacuate passengers down the slide into a wheat field, I felt like Joan of Arc. Maybe a memoir. Someone has already invented Holly Golightly.

Many of the best memory stories have their foundations in guilt or regret. Beginning writers often tend to create heroic characters who represent who they would like to be. Characters with pure hearts who can leap over tall build-ings without splitting their pants don't create the tension and suspense to make readers keep turning the pages. The woman who still thinks her wild days caused her father's death; or the man who regrets having withheld love from his son, especially when he realizes he hadn't done it to make the kid tough, as he had always maintained, he had done it because he enjoyed the power it gave him.

A memory story has more power when the character or the reader has an epiphany provoked by the recollection. What if the reader comes to realize your character could have had the girl he has never gotten over. He had simply lacked the confidence to read the signals she had been sending him. Or what if while telling someone about the father she adored, your character comes to realize he had not been what she had thought at all.

Perhaps your character can find conflict stashed in a year-book, a photo album, an autograph book, a stack of letters tied with a blue ribbon, a box of tarnished medals. An object where memories are stored can flash your character back to the past faster than an airplane flying backward.

If you have no room to stash clutter perhaps one of the following will help you to find a memory for the foundation of your story.

STORY STARTERS

☞ Your character remembers that dreamy summer, when they danced on the dock in the moonlight to "Some Enchanted Evening." It was the only tape he had on the boat, so they played it over and over.

☞ Your character remembers the Halloween costume—a clown suit—she wore the night of the tragedy. They had been trick or treating. Soaping a window was the worst trick they had in mind, but the man in the yellow house had a reputation for being weird. When he fired the shots, your character thought they weren't real . . . until Shawn fell at her feet.

☞ Your character remembers a Sadie Hawkins Day hay ride when he was fifteen. He had never asked a girl for a date. Then the girl with the mouth shaped like a heart asked him. He kissed her, or she kissed him. He wasn't sure. Oh, he loved his wife, but he had never been able to tell her about the night he fell in love with the girl with the heart-shaped mouth. Now he had received an announcement of their tenth-year class reunion. The girl with the heart-shaped mouth was on the planning committee.

☞ Your character remembers his drill sergeant in boot camp. He would still like to knock his block off. Then one night, twenty years later, he sees him standing at the bar.

☞ Your character remembers the first night her sixteen-year-old brother crawled into bed with her in the middle of the night.

☞ Your character remembers the day the judge laid down his sentence, twenty-five to life. He had served ten of them.

☞ Your character remembers the day he said, "I'm sorry. I didn't mean for it to happen, but I love her, and I want a divorce."

☞ Your character looks in the mirror, grimaces, and remembers the day, twenty years ago, when she was crowned Miss America.

☞ Your character remembers the day he said he would disinherit her. She hadn't thought he meant it, but she should have taken him seriously.

☞ Your character remembers the day her only son had called to say, "Mama, I've fallen in love with the most wonderful girl up here. We're going to get married. You'll just love her. Oh, and Mama, she's . . . white."

☞ Your character remember the day the judge said, "I am convinced beyond any reasonable doubt that you are an unfit mother. Therefore, I am awarding the custody of the children to your husband."

☞ Your character remembers the day he read about his wife's affair in *Variety*.

☞ Your character remembers the day, ten years ago, when he said he was going out for a pack of cigarettes. He hadn't even taken a razor.

☞ Your character remembers the day she had crawled under the clothes rack in the department store to hide from her mother . . . just to tease her. When she came out, her mother was gone.

☞ Your character remembers the day the voice on the phone said, "I'm the child you gave up for adoption seventeen years ago."

☞ Your character remembers the first time she saw her father with another woman. She had been eight years old.

☞ Your character remembers her first important role, but mainly she remembers the stage fright that made her feel as if she had been stabbed.

☞ Your character remembers her first time. What a farce.

☞ Your character remembers how much he had hated the baby brother his parents had brought home from the hospital. Not much has changed.

☞ Your character remembers the first rejection letter.

☞ Your character's five older sisters remember when their mother lived with them. They say the mother had to go away because your character had been a colicky baby who cried all the time. Now she is going to visit the mother for the first time. They say your character is not supposed to mention Daddy's friend Amanda who comes for the weekend, and she's not supposed to notice when the mother picks at herself or hides the candy they will take as a present.

☞ Your character remembers when he had to tell his jealous wife his new partner in the squad car was a woman—a young, attractive woman in or out of uniform.

☞ Your character remembers the day the photo had been taken. Some people hadn't died yet. Some had not yet been born.

☞ Your character remembers every item in the trunk—her wedding dress, the christening robe, the letter from his commanding officer who regretted to inform her, the gold star they had sent to hang in her window.

☞ Your character remembers the day the coach said, "You can warm the bench until you're clean."

☞ Your character remembers every time she had worn the red velvet dress.

☞ Your character remembers the phone call. "There has been an accident, a teenage prank that went too far," the officer had said.

☞ Your character remembers another life she led centuries ago when she was one of many other wives in a harem.

☞ Your character remembers when his buddy had called to him for help, but the smoke was so bad and the roof was about to go. He had told the chief he didn't know where the guy could be. There was so much confusion on a five alarm, so no one on his truck had ever doubted him.

☞ Your character remembers when she raised a pig named Pansy and took her to the state fair. When she met a sophisticated boy from town, she had fibbed, saying she had only come to the fair for fun. Pansy hadn't won a blue ribbon. Your character still thinks it might have been the disappointment of her denial that had defeated the pig.

☞ Your character remembers what a hassle he and Charlie had gone through to be able to have the wedding ceremony performed. Now he wishes it hadn't worked in their favor.

☞ Your character remembers how smart his first wife had always looked when they were married. Now at their son's wedding she looked downright shabby.

☞ Your character remembers the disappointment on his father's face when Harvard rejected him, even though his father and his brother were old boy grads.

☞ Your character remembers secretly seducing a girl whose parents were poor and who were the town pariahs. He had been sleeping with her for several months when his parents insisted they go to a restaurant where she waited tables. His mother had said the waitress kept looking at him and asked if he knew her. "Never saw her before in my life," he had said, and the girl had heard him.

☞ Your character remembers his first parachute jump.

☞ Your character remembers when the doctor said, "Your wife is going to be okay, but we weren't able to save the baby. I'm sorry. And you should know, it would not be wise to try again."

☞ Your character remembers the first house they bought. It was an act of faith in their belief that her father would get well.

☞ Your character remembers when, wearing a pea green suit, he interviewed with the managing partner of the firm. The guy had said, "I'll give you a job, if you promise I'll never have to see that suit again."

☞ Your character remembers the Sunday morning he went to church and the minister seemed to be preaching to him, as if he could read his mind and knew the terrible thing your character had done.

☞ Your character remembers when she had become ridiculously infatuated with a star on the soap opera "Days of Our Lives." The only way she could stand to sleep with her husband was to close her eyes and pretend he was the man on the soap.

☞ Your character remembers that one terrible summer, the only time he ever had gone to camp. His mother had waited until he was gone before she told his father to move out.

☞ Reading her mother's letters after her death, your character realizes her mother had always been in love with her father's brother. Then she began to remember fragments of scenes from family gatherings, weekends her mother had gone to visit a friend. . . .

☞   Your character remembers what flashed through his mind when the captain announced the emergency on the intercom and the flight attendant began handing out pillows.

☞   Your character remembers boarding her commuter train as usual. No one expected a terrorist on a train, but there he was shooting at random with what looked like a cap pistol, but what was actually killing people all around her.

☞   Your character remembers the day at Boy Scout camp when he met Joe, who did not follow the code. He even remembers thinking his life would never be the same now that he had met such an exciting and daring guy. What he hadn't realized back then was how disastrous that friendship would be for years to come.

☞   Your character remembers the day she met the man whom she knew immediately she wanted to marry. Her family and even the man told her she would be sorry. She wasn't. What none of them had ever understood what how much she needed to be needed. It made her feel superior and saintly.

☞   Your character remembers the day he stopped loving his wife. They were on a biking trip in the mountains. It had begun to rain. The other bikers pulled out their rain gear. His wife had played helpless, making him feel as if he were responsible for the weather and what she was certain was her imminent death.

☞   Your character remembers the day she stopped trying to be the son whom her mother wanted to replace, the brother who had died in the war. Until that time she had imagined herself like a Shakespearean heroine dressed as a boy, playing the role of a boy. That day she came to realize somewhere along the way in this farce, she had lost her own identity. The first thing she did was book a perm, paint her nails with bloodred polish, and buy a black nightgown.

☞   Your character remembers a suicide that had happened in her hometown when she was young. As she recalls the story as an adult, she begins to think it might not have been what it seemed.

☞   Your character remembers the road he did not take.

CHAPTER 12

Art and Artists

Write stories about what you love, or what you want to learn to love or at least to understand.

If you spend much of your free time going to art museums, attending gallery openings, reading biographies of artists or reviews of shows, why not put your interest and your knowledge into your fiction? Your protagonist could be an artist, someone involved with or related to one. A mean-minded art critic who sets out purposely to ruin a painter's career would make an excellent antagonist. Another possible villain might manage the auction house. Art thieves tend to wear tailor-made suits and live in exotic places. The psyche of an artist who is a fake might be interesting to probe. The toll an aesthete's sensibility takes on her health has possibilities.

Too many overweight women have already looked at a Rubens and sighed for days gone by, but think of the possibilities for plots that begin with your character's reaction to a work of art. A woman sees Michelangelo's "The Creation of

Adam," stares at those glorious legs, the tight stomach laced with taunt muscles, the arms rippling with strength, the sweet face and caring eyes. Even his penis looks like a rosebud. Then her husband, Ralph, brings her out of her trance.

Your shy character discovers Titian's *Venus* when he is an adolescent. The story opens when, at forty and still a bachelor, he continues to search for her face on subway platforms, in the deli, even in his buddies' wives.

Your character had wanted to impress the well educated young man who, on their first date, took her to see a Mondrian exhibit. When he asked her what the blocks of red, blue, and yellow reminded her of, she had said it would make a pretty design for a bolt of gingham. She still thought he might not have been so snooty and so smart if he hadn't known in advance the painting was called *Broadway Boogie Woogie.* He had never called again, but she sometimes went to the gallery on her lunch break when her filing was caught up, just waiting for someone to ask her about it. Now she would say, "Its complex design represents the broken rhythm of jazz," just like the young man had said. She continued to think the pattern would make interesting material for a summer dress, but she sure didn't hear any music.

I know an unlikely, but true story about a woman whose successful husband divorced her when she was in her late fifties and seemed to enjoy finding ways not to pay his support payments. Having decorated several homes in better days, she tried—not very successfully—to build a decorating business. Then one day she saw a painting in one of those big estate-sale warehouses. She pawned some jewelry from her other life to buy the painting, which turned out to be worth many thousands of dollars. Ah, how sweet it is.

Most of us have seen works of art we didn't think we could live without. The longing or the art itself could be the yeast for a story.

I remember two. One hangs in my living room; alas, the other still adorns the wall of a gallery in London. When my former husband and I were young and had more pluck than money, I spotted a large Cornwall seascape that grabbed my heart just as the real crashing surf had done in Maine. I saw the painting in an oh-so-posh gallery window on an oh-so-elegant Bond Street in London. Assuming the pretense of affluent collectors, we drank the oh-so-sophisticated dealer's port, absorbed the dramatic story of the painter's life. To get out of the gallery gracefully, Jack offered a bid—much less than the asking price and much more than we could afford. We had been home about ten days when he called my office to suggest we meet in the park (to revive me in case I passed out, I assume). Our bid had been accepted. the painting was on its way. Its marketplace value has gone up over the years, but not nearly as much as my emotional attachment. Part of my appreciation lies in the story.

DESCRIPTIVE DETAILS

Blue Grass, the work I only *wish* I owned, is a small square of blue and green dots, framed to keep those drops of paint from jumping all over the place.

But how should I tell this story? Where does the dramatic effect lie? I could give more details about the work, hoping to make the reader appreciate the artistry. Or I could focus on the exquisite but small gallery hanging over the entrance to one of London's famed old arcades, which reminded me of a miniature Bridge of Sighs. *Blue Grass* hung opposite a wall of glass open to the architectural splendor of the arcade, as if the building were part of the show.

Another approach would be to concentrate on the joy of seeing the painting as the culmination of one of those rare, wonderful days when the gods seem to be on your side. My friend Karen lives in London. We hadn't seen each other for a year. Bad things had happened to her, but that near perfect day was like an apology. I could concentrate on our pleasure—how almost everything made us laugh, how we had oodles of energy to carry us from one merry experience to the next—excellent seats at the ballet, a captivating French restaurant, the fine exhibition.

I vividly remember two paintings I shall never write about. I adored the primitive gray dappled horse. His rump was too round, his neck a tad short, but he was looking curiously at a tiny mouse hiding in the stall's straw. The other was a portrait of an eighteenth-century dandy wearing a ruff and a hoity-toity expression. He had posed with his hand in such an affected position, we thought he should have a bagel tossed around his second finger, which was extended as if he wanted our attention. One night our apartment burned. My sister, my husband, and I survived, but the paint melted on those canvases, running down like colored rain on a windshield. I felt as if my mare and the dandy had been murdered. I know where to focus the story, but it makes me too sad.

As a writer, your eye must become as sharp as the lens in a camera. You see the entire scene, but recognizing where you should aim the reader's view makes all the difference. Sometimes your character's frayed collar or rumpled suit is a more important detail than the color of his eyes. I think I can remember what Karen and I were wearing the day we saw *Blue Grass,* but our clothes have nothing to do with the story. I once knew a woman in Chicago for whom what we were wearing was always an issue. In retrospect I think she took pleasure in trying to make me feel as if I were wearing a gunny sack . . . and she usually succeeded. But I have no hard feelings, the experience gave me material I haven't even begun to use up.

Cluttering your work with too many details can be as distracting as the artist who heaps image upon image to clutter every inch of the canvas. Adding a dab of color can be important if a sculptor gilds all his work in gold leaf; the blue light from the stained-glass window makes her look like the Madonna; he only uses blood red paint on his canvas. If he paints with a short, always white, feather, or wads up a sweat sock, dips it paint, and dabs the canvas, be sure to include those details.

Finding words to express the familiar in a fresh way, especially when writing about art, will add zest. Describing a ho-hum gray suit as putty-colored, a woman with magnolia skin, a man stroking a cat in his lap, makes your word pictures vivid.

As we discussed earlier, the choice of descriptive verbs can be as effective as modifiers. If your character wins an award, and you say he swaggered or staggered to the podium, we get the picture. If a patron sees a piece sculpted from highly polished stainless steel, commissions the sculptor to do a piece with a similar emotional quality, and for this creation, the artist, on a whim, works with rusty nails, the particulars are vital.

Jewelry designers intrigue me, sometimes for their artistry and sometimes for their audacity. Recently I heard a speech by an attractive woman with long dark hair who unfortunately had a short neck (an essential descriptive detail). She wore a severe black dress. Her only adornment was a necklace made from several square plastic boxes strung close together. When she tilted her head to see the audience in the back of the room, her hair got caught. The large squares with sharp edges made it difficult for her to glance at her notes without injuring her esophagus. I can't remember what she said, but I understand why they call those necklaces chokers.

I would read a story about an American Indian who designed jewelry with allegorical designs. If he liked a customer, he recommended belts, rings, necklaces adorned with symbols of peace and happiness. For testy or arrogant people, he sold them finery created to put a hex on their houses. If you believe in spirits, the conflict for your story could come from how effective the jeweler is at bringing bad luck.

My preference for antique jewelry means I don't need a very large velvet-lined box, but a friend back home had two fishing tackle boxes filled with colorful costume jewelry. "Why do you want to wear an old gold chain that once belonged to some archaic English lady who probably wore funny hats?" my friend once asked, not knowing she had suggested an idea for a story. I visualize the lady who once owned the chain and the delicate watch that no longer runs as having had a trim waist and a creamy bosom. She wore feathers in her hat, buttoned boots, and had a mischievous twinkle in her eye and a sprightly step. I think she bravely sold her jewelry when a tiger attacked her young husband out in India. Tracing her life and telling the tale in flashback from the viewpoint of a woman who felt her presence and influence when she wore the chain a hundred years later could work. Use it if you would like. We couldn't write the same story if we tried.

If she doesn't touch you, perhaps one of the following will arouse your aesthetic sense.

STORY STARTERS

☞ Every day your character went back to the museum, sat in the same spot for hours, and stared at the painting of the woman warrior. The artist had lived two centuries before your character was born, but she knew she had been his subject.

☞ Your character was standing at a coffee bar wearing jeans that were too tight because she had put on weight, when he asked her to model for him. "I'm an artist and I like your butt," he said, and handed her a card. "This address tomorrow at 10 A.M. Ten bucks an hour is all I can pay." She went.

☞ Your character had borrowed a ton of money from his snooty father-in-law to open the Madison Avenue gallery that was losing money as fast as he was losing self-confidence in everything but his insurance policy. The guys he hired for the heist blew it.

☞ Your character believed in her brother's talent, and she loved him, but she simply could no longer afford to pay his bills. She invited him to dinner to explain her predicament. He did not take it well. The story explains the consequences.

☞ The art world knew about her husband's affair with the woman he had been painting in secret before she did. All she had to do was examine the portraits to realize the rumors were true. He had once put that kind of passion into the pictures he had done of her.

☞ He knew he was a genius. If they could not see his talent, they were frogs. He didn't care about their opinion. He couldn't have stopped painting even if he had wanted to. His eyes would not stop seeing. His fingers would not quit, even when the frogs turned off the heat.

☞ Every time your character looked at the huge bronze figure, it made her weep. The story is about discovering the reason for the tears.

☞ The teacher took your character's class to a Dalí exhibit. Your character then was punished when he boiled all the family clocks trying to make them melt, but being grounded didn't cool his ardor. With a Magic Marker, he painted himself a mustache and a goatee, dreamed of glass women with goldfish in their belly. The teacher recommended he see the school psychiatrist.

☞ For months he had done only self-portraits. He could not afford a model. He had no friends who would pose. Actually, he had no friends, no money. One morning he removed the sheet from the almost finished canvas, and what he saw frightened him. He slashed it wildly with a kitchen knife.

☞ They had met and married as promising students at the art institute. Her work had been discovered. His had not, other than "the husband of . . ."

☞ Your character's sister, a painter of birds, moved in. Looking for Popsicles, the kids found black birds in the freezer. Feathers fluttered over the furniture. When your character's husband found droppings in the shower, the family held a war council. What were they to do with the artist who hadn't a sou?

☞ When he won the commission to do the huge sculpture that would stand in the plaza right in the heart of the city, he assumed his reputation was assured. He would be famous. But the public didn't just dislike his work, they hated it, found it offensive. The critics ridiculed it. People spit on it.

☞ Your character, a businessman, had married his wife, an artist, when they were in college. At first her studio was in a barn on the property. Then she turned their living room into a gallery. Slowly the whole house began to be an extraordinarily uncomfortable museum. He began to spend more and more time away from home when meals became beautifully arranged still lifes that seemed to pain her when he ate them.

☞ When your character told his mother he wanted to go to art school instead of medical school, she became hysterical. Picasso was a pig to women; Van Gogh cut off his ear; Dalí was not only a nut case, but a phony one. If he wanted to look at nude women, he should study his anatomy book.

☞ Your character was assigned the task of purchasing the art to decorate the office. Her taste did not please the chairman, the president, the board of directors. How did she expect her colleagues to support her.

☞ Your character, an artist, had had the vision since he was young. He had painted it over and over and over, but never captured on canvas what he saw in his imagination. The dissatisfaction was driving him mad.

☞ Your character's mother was a respected artist and possessed a very strong personality. They had always been very close. His affection for her had given him the respect for women his new wife had found so appealing. He hadn't realized his wife was the jealous type until he took her home to meet his mother. The clash of wills and the irrational behavior from both of them not only astounded him, but put him in the cross fire.

☞ When she disappeared from the home in _____, they found her sleeping at the feet of one of the soldiers at the Korean War Memorial in Washington, D.C. She said the statue was her husband.

☞ He gave your character a replica of an Egyptian snake bracelet alleged to have been designed for Cleopatra. It gave her bad dreams.

☞ Your character went to art school where he did lots of bad Miró imitations, realized he wasn't gifted, and became a quarrelsome critic. Even his friends said he was a devil with an angelic streak, but the devil always won. Trying to be a dispassionate critic was ludicrous. His vengeance, greed, and hatred for those who could do so well what he could not made detachment impossible.

☞ Your character, a psychiatrist, met an artist from Kansas. He painted only bulls. He was very successful. Your character spends time with the artist trying to determine what the artist and his clients found so fascinating about these animals the artist always portrayed as seeming sullen and bored. He, too, became obsessed.

☞ Your character had studied in Paris when he was young. He was a serious painter and worked hard, but his work never attracted attention. Ashamed of having to sell his work to family members in order to eat, one day he attacks a huge canvas with angry splashes of paint, furious strokes made with the wide brush he used to paint the walls of his studio. Worn out, he falls onto the mattress lying on the floor of his loft where he lives, works, and displays his paintings. He awakes to hear the gallery owner he had begged so often to give him a show. "Wake up! You've finally done it! This is fabulous. Such vigor. Such emotion. I want more. We'll do a one man show immediately."

☞ Your character's life was falling apart. Her kids were out of control. Her husband worked seven days a week and was never at home. Paint was peeling off the walls in the living room where there was a leak. Her oven didn't work. The gas tank on her car leaked. That summer she set up an easel in the backyard and began to paint the maple tree. She felt when she had been able to reproduce every line in the bark of the tree, she would have restored order as Nature had intended.

☞ Your character believed toys, especially dolls, were one of many lenses into history. In his shop, he joyfully sold antique toys that evoked stories and memories in the hearts of his customers, but selling a doll was like putting a child out for adoption. He had Eloise, Curious George, Little Prince, Shirley Temple, Princesses Elizabeth and Margaret, beautiful baby dolls, dolls with china heads, dolls stuffed with corn shucks, but his favorite was a Kewpie—the chubby cherub who symbolized our country's lost innocence. He talked to her when no one was around and always found an excuse for not selling her. Then one day a woman came in who said she would pay anything for the sprite. When she was young, the Kewpie . . .

☞ Your character, a brash young man with a lion's confidence, convinced a drinking buddy who happened to be a *New York Times* features writer to do an article about him. He claimed to have earned his art degrees in Europe and to have developed a unique theory that would set a new trend to encompass everyman. He was such a good talker, the response to the article was fantastic. He was interviewed everywhere. "Art is wherever you find it," he said as he led photographers to the fruit and vegetable stand at Dean & DeLuca, the three-tier electronic stock ticker tape in Times Square, the flashing crazy quilt of signs on Forty-second St. Random House had offered him a contract for a book, and he was scheduled to appear on the "Today Show" when the news hit. Your character had escaped from a mental hospital in Rock Island, where he had been confined off and on since he was a child.

CHAPTER 13

_____

Music and Musicians

People's dissimilar taste in music can build thicker walls than an architect could ever construct. Picture a new version of *No Exit:* a rapper forced to listen to Puccini, an opera lover locked in a room with a boom box blasting acid rock. Writers use musical preference as a short cut for character development, tension, and conflict. Imagine a harp player whose son continually practices raucous rock numbers on his bongos in a small apartment, or the rebellious daughter who brings home her fiancé, a country-and-western singer in red cowboy boots who does his own accompaniment on a steel guitar, to her parents who read Emily Dickinson and play violins in a sextet.

What some consider sounds sent from the gods, others call noise. Newspapers abound with complaints that could make interesting stories. Noise gives demure pacifists machine-gun dreams. Sixty decibels penetrating one's walls allows a sufferer to call the police. Zoning laws permit people who run clubs to declare sound turf.

When you slip into the viewpoint of a character, you usually can find something to like. To improve my disposition on the city streets, I've often considered writing a story from the point of view of a bored, suburban kid with a snazzy stereo-equipped car, who for kicks comes into Manhattan to get a rise out of the natives. He has to be from the suburbs, or maybe the boroughs. New York kids don't have cars. Where would they park? When he crosses the bridge, the kid, who is to become my character, preens in the mirror before he slips in the CD, turns the volume to the top, and rolls down the windows—even in the winter. As he glides up and down the avenues (too much traffic on the crosstown streets), little old ladies clasp their ears; dogs howl; mothers wag their fingers; men shake their fists; but girls give him the eye. I haven't figured out what happens to my character, but if you have an idea, you can have him. I might just buy ear plugs.

Don't overlook the business side of music. *New York Times* reporter Allan Kozinn recently said: "Like the gods in Wagner's 'Ring' cycle, the producers who ran the big classical record labels in the 1950's created their own Valhalla, a shimmering fortress in the musical heavens, fit for the heroes of song and stage—the Callases, Heifetzes, Horowitzes, and Toscaninis—and built with treasure wrested from their pop divisions. It was generally agreed back then, that this arrangement preserved something crucial in Western civilization. But by the 1970's, when the fortunes of pop labels dwarfed those of the classics, a generation of number crunchers had seized the corporate reins."

Tell me about it. New York's mayor tells me I live in the Culture Center of the World, but if I ever move to Maine all year round it will be because on Bailey Island I can listen to four classical music stations—with fewer talky announcers—twenty-four hours per day.

One morning a few years ago, several New Yorkers—including this one—thought aliens had invaded our sound systems. I flipped on the radio set to the classical station I turned on every day, even before my computer. Ohmigod! Some crazy person was pounding the devil out of something or someone in there, and screeching the same thing over and over and over . . . maybe "Baby, love me, baby, love me, baby, love me"? Surely not. I fiddled and fiddled with the dial. That one was broken. Found another radio . . . it too had gone berserk. Before I did, someone called to tell me the sneaky station had switched to alternative rock over night. To avoid flack from classical music lovers, they had made the switch without announcement or warning.

I'm only beginning to see the humor in this incident. If you can use it, take it.

If you can't find a touching story in what has happened to the classical performers or the people who produced their work, you might try for irony. Imagine a down-on-his-luck classical violinist reading the titles of *Billboard*'s bestsellers.

Some of the misogynous, abusive rap lyrics I have seen in print give me the creeps. Fortunately, I hardly ever hear them because I usually can't understand what they are saying, but I respect the First Amendment more than I abhor the message. If I were to write a story about the conflict between the musicians and the Religious Right censors, the gangster rappers would be my protagonists. Finding the means to present a sympathetic character whose values are deplorable, now there's a challenge.

Operatic villains and heroes almost always have an abundance of dramatic dash. Since the time of Gluck, opera composers have considered their works primarily as vehicles for the dramatic stage-good stories revealed by singing actors with the assistance of an orchestra. As we discussed in Twice- and Thrice-Told Tales, artists have always borrowed from each other. Movie plots are often based on novels, paintings have inspired characters, but the opera composers especially have turned to other sources to find good books for their music. Wagner went mostly to the powerful Norse myths, Gounod used the legend of Faust, Puccini's *Madame Butterfly* and *Tosca* were based on popular dramatic hits of the day, Bizet found Carmen's story in a French novelette. In an about-face, Jonathan Larson, a young East Village artist, borrowed Puccini's libretto for *La Bohème* and adapted it into the 1996 Broadway hit *Rent*. You might be inspired by some of the highly charged operatic tales such as the bizarre story of love and revenge in *Il Trovatore* or the swift-running comedy in *The Marriage of Figaro*.

Even though I never mastered my clarinet to the extent

I could make the notes sound the way they were written, to say nothing of playing around with them, I believe jazz musicians and writers think alike: "What if" I played it differently, wrote it not the way you would expect? When we're blowing him to the cemetery, what if I mixed a little hallelujah joy in the blues . . . what if in my story he's only pretending to be dead and the casket is filled with rocks?

Blues, the heart of jazz, is the conflict, the complications writers must put in a story. Jazz lyrics are earthy and concerned with basic human problems—love and sex, poverty and death—the material for stories. The jazz tempo, like the tone of fiction, may vary and the mood range from total despair to cynicism and satire.

Jazz themes grew from political and historical roots as vivid, as painful, and as true as *War and Peace, The Red Badge of Courage* and *Gone With the Wind.* It's a musical expression of African-American culture developed from black work songs, field shouts, sorrow songs, hymns, and American Negro spirituals. Just as a writer draws from what she sees, hears, and experiences, and then creates a character to tell a story reverberating in her head, a jazz artist's harmonic, rhythmic, and melodic elements are spontaneous, emotional, and improvisational. He finds sounds to express his soul. You can feel the suffering, experience the joy, see the people, hear the tales that musicians tell. If luck's a lady, your stories will do the same.

TENSION AND SUSPENSE

Writers who make stories to be read, not seen or heard except in the mind, work so much harder than those who write for movies, television, and radio. Their audiences do, too. Describing a rubber-limbed, hip-hop rapper bopping to a boom box beat on a street corner, noisy as a war zone, where his kid brother passes his ball cap with one hand while holding up his too large, hand-me-down pants with the other, is not the difficult part. Give a few descriptive details, create an appropriate metaphor, provide a perceptive simile, and your reader can visualize the scene. She is there. Have the little kid grin and do a deep bow to the lady who tosses in a fiver, and the boy in the too-big pants has probably touched the reader's heart. But even though she has a sympathetic attachment to the spunky child, there has to be more threat than his losing his trousers to keep her turning the pages. The writer will have to create tension and suspense to maintain her interest.

As a plot progresses, it has to arouse various expectations about the future course of events. The reader has to have an anxious uncertainty about what is going to happen to the characters she likes or to those who have sparked her curiosity. Radio, movie, and television writers can rely on the soundtrack for help. The tempo of the music indicates what is coming and how you are to feel about it. Think of the background beat in a car chase, when a tornado approaches, when the bus is out of control, when the bad guy is about to snatch the child, when the heroine is fighting the rapist.

You have to create the pace, the rhythm, and the anxiety with appropriate language and sentence structure. If a lunatic climbs up on a nearby statue to take a potshot at the kid losing his jeans, the pacing should be quick. This is not the place to write a Henry James–length sentence meticulously describing his actions, thoughts, sensibility, and country of origin. The language should be as harsh and ugly as the act. The sound of gritty words, like "grunt," "grovel," "snout," "snoot," "smack," "whack," and "wham," becomes the soundtrack. If the bullet hits the boy, the mood must change. The soundtrack would switch to something sweet and sentimental. The writer, however, must find lyrical, poetic language that avoids the maudlin but expresses the slow, sorrowful pace of grief. The reader should feel the strangers on the street mourning the loss of joy.

If what happens in a story violates our expectations, the interplay between surprise and suspense increases the magnetic power of a plot. The incident above depends upon action for the tension, but in the most memorable stories like *Hamlet*, the suspense grows out of character. If Hamlet had not been superstitious and religious, he would have killed his uncle immediately, married Ophelia, and Gertrude would have lived to be a grandmother. We are surprised the first time he has an opportunity to do the deed but doesn't. His rationalization is he would be sending

Claudius to heaven because the king was saying his prayers. But then we remember what has gone before. Hamlet has been afraid his father's ghost might have been sent by the devil. He considers suicide, but doesn't act because he believes his soul would go to hell. His character has been developed so clearly in the beginning, even though the reader is at first startled when Hamlet doesn't act to rid the kingdom of evil as she wishes, upon reflection, she realizes, yes, of course, that is exactly what the young prince would do, or in this case, not do.

To write a powerful story about the kid in the hand-me-down pants above, start with developing his character. What characteristics set him apart, like Hamlet's religious faith, Ophelia's jealousy, Ahab's obsession. Let's call the boy Spunky and make him fearless—an admirable, appealing trait. Set it up by showing he is not afraid of the dark, or of the big tough guys on the block. Then just imagine the trouble this trait can lead him into. You will be able to create so much tension and suspense, your reader will stay up all night to find out what happens to the little dickens. Without that desire to know how things turn out, you don't have a story.

STORY STARTERS

☞ To help pay for her studies, your character, a music student, volunteered to be a page turner for performing musicians. Then a cellist asked that she be fired. The page turner was to be unobtrusive, unnoticed by the audience, he argued. But how could someone with golden tresses—masses of cascading gold lace—skin like heavy cream, narrow hips and thighs, hands like lilies . . . how could someone with that grace and beauty be invisible? Yes, she was good at her job, but she was distracting the audience, he said.

☞ Your character could only listen to the dj's cultured voice, smooth as chocolate mousse, in the middle of the night when for eight hours she played soothing, sentimental music that dreams were made of. When she talked about the music, she spoke in the tone women used to whisper in a lover's ear. Mad for her, your character waits, at dawn—the end of her shift—outside the radio station where she works.

☞ At 5'2" your brash character gave up any hope of bouncing a basketball out of the ghetto. He would become a Hip-Hop Entrepreneur, like some of his friends. He changed his name from Jason Simons to Inyaface and found the craziest crackrock user in the hood. Inyaface recorded what the man said when he was high, and wrote a couple of songs. He rounded up a few guys who sang in the school chorus, got his girlfriend to design a group logo and they were ready to roll.

☞ Your character managed to get backstage after the group's last performance. On the couch in the swaggering lead singer's dressing room, she spotted a tattered teddy bear with one eye missing.

☞ For performers, ego is usable, if not necessary, capital. Any overabundance had flowed into the personalities of the members of the symphony, except for your character, the pianist. He shed his grand manner as quickly as he doffed his concert tails to become a self-effacing guy next door. The press loved him, but the conflict comes from the resentment felt by the other musicians. One of them plants an ugly rumor with the media.

☞ Your character hadn't seen her for ten years, but one night he went into a bar where a vocalist was singing a ballad. "My god, that was our song," he said, and everything that had happened began to flow through him all over again.

☞ Nobody listened to the heartache stuff your character's mama used to sing in Nashville with Johnny Cash, Merle Haggard, Willie Nelson. He gathered up some of the other kids whose parents were "used-to-be" great country singers and went to Branson, Missouri, where it was happening now. They added steel guitars, drums, and darkened the subject matter. His mother stopped taking his calls after his first hit.

☞ Your character plays first violin for the symphony. It is his life. He has no wife, no family, no pets, no friends off the stage. Then a throwaway child, a five-year-old girl, parks on the stoop of his brownstone and refuses to go away.

☞ Your character tries to become the crooner her mother had

been. At first they said she was a chip off the old block-buster, but then life began to interfere with her art.

☞ All of your character's close college friends were in the marching band with him. He missed his first trip when he came down with a bad case of the flu. They were on a chartered bus going to the out-of-town football game when the accident happened. Some were killed; most of them hurt in some serious way. That was the day your character came to know himself.

☞ When your character—a Broadway musical diva—had recordings high on the charts, a reporter once called her a Shirley Temple with a touch of Betty Boop. He said her cupid-bow lips dispensed genuine sweetness, while her piles of frizzy curls and Vargas girl figure courted a bomb-shell image. The press had adored her back then, but that had been nine or ten years ago, before her personal life had hit the skids and she had been unable to perform. Your story begins with her comeback.

☞ Your character used to be so proud to say she had married a composer. That was when she still believed the public would come to appreciate what he called his "happy art." At first she had "sensed the sensation"—his goal—when he did his trick with the dance of shifting rhythmic steps, the cascading of one canonic line following another to a fluorescent harmonic shimmer—his description. Tired of supporting him, now she was having an affair and wished she could drop her husband off somewhere, as you could when you had a pet you no longer wanted.

☞ Your character, a crooner, thought they were playing his exit music; then some kids, thinking he was camp, picked him up. His family whispered "second childhood," but he was having the time of his life. Heroic or pathetic? Your call.

☞ In the seventies your character was the main man/disco dude who got 400 women's phone numbers in one single calendar year. The world belonged to the suave, smooth-talking guy who had a steady gig mixing wax and eight-tracks for one of the canopic clubs. They came swarming in like cockroaches. Then it was all over. Now he looks in the mirror and sees a heartthrob frozen in time.

CHAPTER 14

Professions and Just Plain Jobs

If you have never been sure what you wanted to be when you grew up, or even if you wanted to grow up, becoming a writer could be the most intelligent decision you have ever made. You can pretend to be a plumber, a pilot, a politician. Without wrecking your résumé, you can change professions in every story if you wish. No one will call you a job hopper. Writing and acting have similarities, but a writer doesn't have to be young, handsome, and unafraid to kiss strangers or sing and dance in front of a crowd of people to play roles other than the one he was awarded at birth.

During the Age of Aquarius, most youth thought what they wanted to do was save the world. But they also wanted to know *why* they wanted to save the world. I'm so glad I didn't miss the sometimes wonderful, sometimes wacky things that could only have happened in the late sixties and early seventies. At that time psychotherapist Carl Rogers wrote *On Becoming a Person,* a book destined to become a popular tool in determining why people chose their careers. The University of Chicago, an institution that has always taken everything serious seriously, made no exception with Rogers. I remember a psychology class where we imperiously concluded elementary teachers chose to teach little kids because they were Peter Pans, and therapists chose their field because they had never had a meaningful personal relationship. I felt terribly superior, until, by the same process, the group determined I could never be a successful follower. At that age, the possibility of finding anyone who wanted to play follow the leader with me seemed bleak.

At this stage of my life, I'm simply so glad to file with the IRS as a writer that I no longer try to determine why I do it, but Rogers's process comes in handy when assuming the viewpoint of a character who might be a cowboy, a cook, or a crook.

POINT OF VIEW

THIS IS IMPORTANT. Point of view refers to the outlook from which the events in a novel or short story are related. Picture a big-city street corner at five P.M. Listen to the noise. Watch the action. Now switch from what you see and hear to look at the city's rush-hour traffic through the eyes of:

a bike messenger
a teenager with a Walkman
a person in a wheelchair
a businessman late for a
  meeting
an EMS ambulance driver
a delivery truck driver
an out-of-state big-rig driver
a mother with three cranky
  kids

a lost child
a chauffeur
a street performer
a Rollerblader
a fire truck driver
a traffic cop
a city bus driver
a blind person

None of the above are experiencing the same thing. Even if they're standing so close they can feel each other's heartbeats, they see, hear, and feel a different scene. That is called point of view.

Deciding from whose perspective your story will be told is a major decision that will lock you into a tone, style, and diction for the entire process. Think how your decision will affect the plot and the theme.

First-Person Viewpoint

The story is told by one of the characters himself, who may be the protagonist, as Dickens's David Copperfield. The bike messenger might say, "I don't sweat it, dude. Learned my job dodgin' cars playin' stick ball in the Brooklyn streets. Cars ain't the problem, man. People is. The main thing's not to stop if you should happen to hit someone. Should look where they're going. That's the way I see it."

Electing for your character to speak directly to the reader is a more intimate experience, but if you choose first person, all action must be seen or heard by your character in his vernacular and tone. You can't switch point of view, even if you would like for the biker's mother to say things she would never say in his presence. The biker could be behind the door listening to what his mother says, but "overheard" techniques can seem contrived.

Third-Person Narration

More often, the author tells the story from the viewpoint of one character, restricting the reader to her field of vision and range of knowledge. The major switch is from "I" to "she," but narrative summary usually seems less intrusive from the third person. The "she" can be a major or a minor character or a mere witness. Here is how the traffic snarl might affect another character on that corner:

Jane Brooks had only been driving an EMS ambulance for three months. She had taken the job to punish herself for flunking out of medical school. When she hit traffic with a patient in back, her left eye always began to twitch, but what really upset her was having a relative, like this patient's husband, screaming directions at her.

In this instance, the husband's angry language can show

how he feels about Jane's driving, but you can't go into his thoughts. The reader experiences what is happening only as Jane sees, feels, and thinks.

Omniscient Point of View

The author tells the story moving from character to character and event to event, having free access to the motivation, thoughts, and feelings of his characters, and introducing information to the reader when and where he chooses. Beginning writers often find the omniscient viewpoint tempting, but even though it is less restricting, it is more difficult to grip the reader when he doesn't identify with one character. The traffic scene could be told as follows:

When the big-rig driver winked at her, for just a second Mira Morgan felt like jumping into the cab and running away from the crowds and the children who were behaving like such brats. Mike, the trucker, would have welcomed Mira's company, but forget the kids. The biggest one reminded him of his Jake back in Tennessee—the one who had a thing about matches. All Charlie Ferry wanted to do was get out of his traffic mess, drop his last load of fish, and head home over the bridge. He started the honking and Mike and everyone joined in when that damned cop held them through another light just to let the guy in the wheelchair cross. Mira, Charlie, and the trucker would have been even more incensed if they could have known how much the cop enjoyed the chaos. Controlling all these people made him feel like God.

The point of view you select shapes your story. Republicans don't think like Democrats. A girl doesn't see the same world as the boy walking in lockstep beside her. Age, gender, experience, race, religion, geography, attitude shape the way characters view the world. As narrator, you have to cast your perspective aside to become that person, to see, feel, and think as she does.

Your character's career or job also shapes your story. The work your character does limits his experience and affects his language. Architects, bakers, surgeons, strippers, literature professors, thieves, all sprinkle their con-

versation and thoughts with metaphors that reflect what
they do.

If you want to write a novel with a business setting, unless you have run a company, or have been close to someone who has, it is best not to promote yourself to
chairman. Stratosphere affects the view and the way one
uses and feels about power. A manager's or an administrative assistant's perspective can give an ironic, comic, or
sympathetic twist to what goes on in those impressive
glass-and-steel skyscrapers.

The emphasis on showing a politically correct viewpoint
has distorted more fiction with potential than any other
issue in my lifetime. No sensitive, intelligent writer wants
to promote race, religion, or gender bias, but in my opinion
we have gone over the edge. Not all the physically or
mentally handicapped have stiff upper lips and face life's
difficulties heroically. Not all women are morally and in-
tellectually superior to men; not all ghetto kids have an IQ
of 140. When you're writing a credible story and suddenly
think you had better change the sex or the skin color or
manufacture a character or an incident to show your im-
partiality, it's going to be as obvious as a bumper sticker.
Strive for truth as you see it. You might find a courageous editor.

If you are bored with the way you make your living, or
feel burned out, now you have the opportunity to change
careers with each book or story. Perhaps you will want to
step into the shoes of one of the following:

STORY STARTERS

☞ Your character was a bareback rider under the big top. She
wore spangles on her costume, and trumpets sounded
when she rode into the ring. She loved the ringmaster, but
he loved the clown who had big feet even when she wasn't
in costume.

☞ Your character has lived a lavish lifestyle for thirty years.
Oh sure, he'd had to change his identity a few times, but
that was half the fun of being a con man. Now the CIA
was closing in on his yacht.

☞ Two convent schools had tossed out your flamboyant character. When she married the older well-known paleoanthropologist, she didn't even have a high school diploma. She, a quick study, went with him on field trips until she learned the ropes. Then she divorced him, used her impressive settlement to set up her own research team. When she began to receive more acclaim than her former husband, he stopped working in the field and devoted his time to writing in order to destroy her reputation. He said she hogged the limelight when they worked together, accused her of sloppy fieldwork.

☞ Burnout? Your character felt fried, boiled pink, and peeled, but he had a mortgage and a family that lived a tad above his means. The only thing he had ever done was sell. Then he had a fabulous idea.

☞ Her father died and your character inherited the profitable funeral home that had been in the family for three generations, but she wanted to be a race-car driver.

☞ To please his editor, your character, a reporter, had to find or invent the story his boss wanted. That meant he had to put his ethics on hold.

☞ By the time he became the CEO of a Fortune 500 company, he felt entitled to the power and the perks. Your character, his administrative assistant, lives vicariously.

☞ Since graduating from college, your character worked for the IRS, processing claims for stupid snakes who made six- and seven-figure incomes. He made $35,000. When he decided to make their lives miserable he began to enjoy his work. His colleagues often heard demonic "hee, hee, hees," coming from his cubicle.

☞ Your character, an elfish-looking small man with a comfortable belly and holes in the elbows of his old cardigan, had run a bookstore for forty years without becoming too involved with people outside the pages of his books. Then a frightened young couple began spending more and more time with him, telling him their bizarre story. Unwittingly, he became involved in protecting them. Then he began to feel as if *he* needed protection.

☞ What if your character were a good man who becomes so

distraught by the unfairness of it all, he becomes a hit man to bring justice to the world.

☞ What if your character became a nanny for twins she grew to love so much she kidnapped them because their parents were too stupid to appreciate them as she did.

☞ Megan, your character, grew up with Patrick, Shawn, Ian, and Joey. She had always hung out with them, not the other girls in the neighborhood. In their teens, when the guys began to do a few jobs—liquor stores, gas stations, convenience stores (never in the parish), she was their lookout. Who was going to suspect a pretty girl loitering around? When Patrick was hit, the others realized Megan wasn't just one of the guys. She had always been in love with Patrick.

☞ Your character had been on the force for four years when he was chosen to be one of the firehouse hunks on the calendar they were making to support charities. When it came out with the ad line "Oh, to Be Young, Brave and Shirtless," his life changed. The soaps and a modeling agency called. He did not handle the attention well, and the guys turned on him.

☞ Your character is a priest who loses his faith.

☞ Your character lands a position in a profitable company, but very soon learns there's no way to stay clean and work for people who make their money in such devious ways.

☞ Your character owns a horse that wins the Kentucky Derby. Then the rumor begins that the jockey gave the horse a drug. The jockey claims the owner told him to do it.

☞ Your character is a fact checker for a popular, glossy magazine. She discovers a big star has lied in the interview for a piece the magazine is about to run. The star offers her a hard-to-refuse bribe.

☞ Your character is a young nun. A Giants baseball player falls in love with her.

☞ Your character, a department head in state government, makes a political enemy in human resources. Direly understaffed, he finally gets approval to add three people. His enemy sends him three problems, but it could be considered politically incorrect to fire or reject any of the three.

☞ Your character is a stringer for a big-city newspaper. The big story practically drops in his lap. All he has to do is betray his source.

☞ Your character becomes the favorite waitress at The Lonelyhearts Café because she's so unwittingly bad at it.

☞ Your character must have had some means of income, but no one knew for sure just what it was. He was best known as the person everyone wanted as a dinner guest. He had a truffle hound's nose for sniffing out private metropolitan pleasure domes described in colors entirely his own. His Proust-like instincts about the foibles and intricacies of the people around him ideally equipped him to be a gregarious storyteller of often unprintable gossip, astringent and wicked, charming and modest to the point of insecurity. His lack of pomposity made him unique among those on his circuit.

☞ Your character's father had been a ward boss. When she decided to run for office, she cashed in his chits.

☞ Your character had begun to take tap and ballet lessons when she was five. Immediately, her teacher not only recognized her exceptional talent, but was impressed by the dedication and discipline shown by such a youngster. By the time she was fifteen she was performing with a ballet company and completing high school by correspondence. She danced for three decades. When she realized she would soon be unable to perform, she panicked. She had devoted herself to intense training since she was a child and as an adult had gone on taking orders from choreographers and rehearsal masters. Now, she was supposed to be an adult. Who was going to tell her what to do and how to do it?

☞ Your character, a window trimmer for department stores, was madly—her friends said obsessively—in love with an ambitious young lawyer. He had always worked long hours, but your character had begun to think it was ruse he used to spend time with other women. After a hard sale, she gets the job of decorating the windows of a store across from his apartment building. After hours, she removes the mannequin dressed in a scanty outfit from the cruise collection. Even though it is snowing outside and the store heat has been turned down, she puts on the shorts and halter, and takes the doll's place. About midnight, the love of her life walks by with a redhead. Your character . . .

☞ Your character is a marriage counselor. When he falls in love with the wife of one of his clients, he begins to play dirty.

☞ When he was young, your character had been a stunt pilot who performed at air shows, but for the past several years he had been a commercial airline pilot. Each week he flew one layover trip LAX-JFK-LAX and one Chicago turn-around. Bored to the point of paralysis, one day he decides to see what the small jet he's flying will do. He rolls the baby with a full load of passengers.

☞ Your character is a pastor for a city church with a large, sophisticated congregation. His parishioners don't demand hellfire and damnation sermons, but rather want to be made to feel there is order in the universe. For a challenging diversion, he invents things in his basement, usually practical things like kitchen utensils and objects to help him organize the garage and workshop. Then he invents something he feel turns against him. He keeps hurting himself, the contrapaction is capable of doing more than he intended. He begins to think the devil, whom he hasn't thought about in a long time, has inspired it.

The following is a list of characters whose viewpoints could be interesting. You supply the plot:

☞ A bingo caller
☞ A chef
☞ A stuntman
☞ A legendary country-and-western singer
☞ A librarian in a small town
☞ A bored, but retired FBI agent
☞ A mechanic in the race car pits
☞ A gardener on a big estate
☞ A crossword puzzle designer
☞ A hired gun
☞ A noted food critic who developed allergies
☞ A clammer on a small island
☞ A nosy postmistress in a village

☞ A pediatrician in an affluent community
☞ A cattle rancher who feared mad cow disease
☞ A blackjack dealer in a casino
☞ A checker in a bustling supermarket
☞ A security guard in the diamond district
☞ A real estate developer in a historic area
☞ An editor for a fashion magazine
☞ A hand model
☞ A person who does voice-overs
☞ A hacker
☞ A TV preacher
☞ A manicurist
☞ A career master sergeant
☞ An over-the-hill anchorman
☞ An inventor
☞ An aide to the President of the United States
☞ A terrorist
☞ The captain of a cruise ship
☞ A shoe salesman
☞ A flight attendant who had flown for twenty years
☞ The president of a small unendowed college that desperately needs funds
☞ The super in a small walk-up building in a poor neighborhood
☞ The doorman at the swankiest hotel in the city
☞ The publicist for an egotistical bestselling author
☞ The villain in a popular sitcom
☞ The layout person for a porn magazine
☞ The head nurse in the emergency room in an inner-city hospital that is not the setting for a television show
☞ The accountant for the wealthiest man in the world
☞ The chairman of a quite successful company that makes and sells controversial products like firearms, box cutters, cigarettes, liquor
☞ An air controller, who goes berserk, in a busy airport
☞ A once-famous blues singer performing in a subway station

CHAPTER 15

Travel

Anne Tyler's protagonist Macon Leary hated to travel, but he made his living writing *Accidental Tourist* guidebooks with logos of a comfortable armchair with wings. His ideal reader was the businessman abroad who longed for a king-size Beautyrest in Madrid, a taste of Sweet'n Low in Tokyo, and a restaurant in Rome that would serve Chef Boyardee. In *The Last Thing He Wanted,* Joan Didion's Elena McMahon doesn't bother to pack a toothbrush when she sets out for a turnaround trip to the Caribbean from which she never returns.

Note the plot twists in both novels. A story about a perfect Hawaiian holiday would be as much fun as watching Harry and Gilda's slides from their last trip. How your character, in his short-sleeved shirt, reacts when the plane is forced to make an emergency landing in Minneapolis just before a blinding ice and snow storm hits, has possibilities.

In an earlier chapter, we looked at ways to describe settings, to use places to create an ambiance that has an effect on your character. Here the spotlight turns to the act of traveling, the effect moving about has on your character, what impact the people he encounters make, the consequences the change in place has on the plot. Make the slightest alteration in his character or circumstances and the difference influences your narrative, just as your life story would not be the same if your father had been rich or you had been born without a thumb.

A man wearing tropical clothes in a Minneapolis blizzard makes different decisions than the same man on a sandy beach playing a ukulele. Imagine the consequences if you modified the situation in any of the following ways:

☞ To pay for the trip your character has used the maximum credit allowed on his cards.

☞ Before they land one of the other passengers—he doesn't know who—has picked his pocket.

☞ Your character was going to Hawaii to celebrate his eighty-seventh birthday.

☞ Your character, a single father, had planned this trip in an effort to recover from the death of his only child.

☞ Your character made his living as a stand-up comic.

No one had more fun poking fun at himself, the people, and the places he visited than Mark Twain. The Connecticut Yankee at King Arthur's Court says, "Whenever the literary German dives into a sentence, that is the last you are going to see of him till he emerges on the other side of the Atlantic with his verb in his mouth." In *Innocents Abroad*, he says, "They spell it Vinci and pronounce it Vinchy; foreigners always spell better than they pronounce."

A word of caution when attempting to re-create colloquial speech patterns or dialect. Few have had Twain's ear for idioms. Spelling things funny usually confuses. Trying to write Southern after only traveling through Georgia listening to the radio in your pickup truck probably won't work. It might be better to allow the character washin' down Moon Pies with slugs of warm Dr Pepper to play a minor role but to write from the viewpoint of someone who talks more like you. If you train yourself to listen and to carry a notebook, you will be able to introduce those who add local color to a story set somewhere else, but after a two-week holiday you probably won't be able to sustain the perspective for three hundred pages. Language reflects thought, and Texans don't think or talk like people from Maine any more than the Irish speculate and speak as the English.

When you begin to think like a writer, you realize you don't have to fly with the astronauts to get a new perspective. A stroll to the corner for the newspaper can become material. At the newsstand, a weeping woman could be watching a car drive away fast. Or remember the hostess of the beach house who kept you working—walking the bad-tempered dog and her bratty kids—from the moment you arrived, the bed and breakfast with the mouse in the down comforter, the day you took the wrong turn in the South of France and didn't find your hotel again for two days. All of it—the feelings, the frustrations, the ambiance—can be worked into a story you create about someone else with a life experience different or more dramatic than yours. Remember: *Write from experience not about it.*

A character lurking in my notebook used to have three faces, but he has melted into the composite innkeeper somewhere in the British Isles. The first real one, a garrulous Irishman, bought a large hunting lodge, then claimed he couldn't keep it up without taking in paying guests part of the year, but frankly I think he simply wanted an audience for his tall tales. The second, a gregarious Scot, which sounds like a contradiction in terms, said when he found the most beautiful spot on the Scottish Coast he felt selfish not sharing it. The third had been an antique dealer and a food critic until he found a lovely house in the Lake District and became a loquacious host. All three of them had found a lucrative, captured audience.

My gabby innkeeper will tell a dramatic story—probably about something mysterious that happened to one of his previous guests. He will only be a witness/narrator, but of course his point of view can't help but shade the tale. I imagine his tone—perhaps use of hyperbole—might make him a less-than-reliable narrator, which adds tension to tales.

Traveling to an eerie setting, like an unfriendly foreign

village where everyone pretends not to understand what your character says, but she senses they do, could portend trouble for your protagonist.

Recently a friend received an invitation to a wedding for a Saudi princess. Fortunately, she knew someone at the embassy who taught her the ropes, but I've been thinking "what if" an innocent American went to such an affair and did not know only harlots wore pants—even silk Armani pants—or short sleeves, even when the temperature reached one hundred degrees. I can imagine a painful, but humorous scene when the character didn't understand the tea ritual, which ends with guests being doused with scent—a tradition left over from before the invention of air-conditioning, when even the wealthy did not smell like lilacs.

Think of a story woven together with substance and shadow—what your character knows and what she imagines. Picture a scene where your protagonist lands in an out-of-character situation, such as having to walk across the desert in high-heeled slippers, a sissy who has to drive a dogsled across a frozen lake, someone who has to try to land a plane from radio instructions. If you spend a lot of time at the movies, try to forget the over-the-edge Hollywood stuff like an extraordinarily precocious kid left home alone, the city slicker sentenced to a horse ranch, the hero pole-vaulting over tall buildings without splitting his trousers. Even when you see it you don't believe it. Keep the illusion in your story.

CAUSE AND EFFECT

Most great literary works are character-driven, no matter where the story takes place. Raskolnikov kills an old woman with an ax. Dostoyevsky describes the act in a few pages. He spends hundreds of pages examining the effect of the act on his protagonist and the other characters.

Huckleberry Finn breaks down when Twain shifts the focus from Huck's losing his innocence to the antics of con men, feuding families, and Tom Sawyer's silliness.

In South Africa your character loses her purse with her

credit cards, money, passport, and travel checks. What results? If your purpose is to reveal the spoiled or dependent side of this woman, you spotlight her anguish, the mistakes she makes. If you see her as tough and resourceful, she shows her strength of character through her decisions, the canny way she persuades bureaucrats to break the rules, the price she pays for getting herself out of the jam.

Before you write a scene, the question is: What do I want to accomplish here? If she loses her money and identity, what effect will it have on my character? Will showing her strength be productive in moving my plot toward the climax, or has her courage or the lack of it already been established? As suspenseful as the incident could be, if it doesn't fit the plan or reveal something the reader doesn't already know about the protagonist, forget it. Put it in your notebook to use in another story.

When you examine cause and effect, the simple act of leaving the comfort of home might create a story if you have developed a reclusive character burdened with fears and doubts who is forced by circumstances to sally forth reluctantly. Most of us blithely hand our luggage over to a skycap, but imagine the anguish of someone who does not understand or does not trust the system. Picture this discombobulated person in a crowded airport: the lounge is littered with sticky take-out containers, cranky children, angry travelers screaming in many tongues; then the plane she did not trust in the first place has been delayed for mechanical difficulty—like faulty flaps—which she cannot make head nor tails of.

If you have an urge to go back to Venice, to walk once again on the sand in Tahiti, to go barging on the Seine, but you can't afford it, create a character to send. Being able to write a story taking place in the setting you can't forget is one of the myriad rewards for a writer. Of course, you now realize, you can't send him off on a fantasy spin. His adventure has to have a beginning, a middle, and an end. Something has to happen. What happens has to mean something. What happens has to have an effect on your character.

Try one of these trips to see where it might take you and your character:

STORY STARTERS

☞ Your character, who was not athletic or in good shape, joined the bike trip because she loved Frank. On the third day he began to pretend he didn't know her.

☞ Your character went to the company's sales conference in the Caribbean, hoping to score some points with his boss. Then they went deep-sea fishing, and your character caught the biggest sailfish ever landed in those waters. The look on his boss's face blew this thrill of success away.

☞ White water rafting had seemed like an ideal vacation when she read the brochure. Your character felt nothing but terror from the first day. Then she began to realize one of the others had taken an intense dislike to her.

☞ Your character, a father of five, knew he was taking a chance when he decided to ski the trickiest slope. When he fell, he felt the snap in his back.

☞ Your character went to Israel to get in touch with her roots. What happened was she fell in love with a young, handsome Palestinian.

☞ Your character had lived in the ghetto until he won a scholarship to an elite Eastern prep school. Now he didn't fit in any place.

☞ At sixteen few kids got on well with their parents, but things were especially tense between your character and her parents. When she signed up as an exchange student, they all thought it might be a good idea. None of them could have imagined she would never come home.

☞ When crossing the wide street with lots of traffic, your character looked the wrong way. Two days later, the tour guide located the hospital where they took her. She did not remember her name or the words that used to be her language.

☞ Your character was hitchhiking across the country when a female big-rig driver picked him up.

☞ Your character takes a vacation to Singapore with her best friend. This is the first time they have traveled together. They share a hotel room, have meals with each other. When they get off the plane back in the States, your character says, "I never want to see you again as long as I live." The friend says, "You'll never have a chance."

☞   Your character's company sends him to Tokyo for several weeks. Bored, lonely, and a tad homesick, he picks up a woman in a bar. It wrecks his life.

☞   Your character goes to the blue room on the plane headed for Madrid. When she opens the door, she sees the back of a terrorist holding a machine gun.

☞   Your character had been reading a book about people in the Depression who had moved around the country by hopping freights. On a whim she climbed into an empty freight car and off she went.

☞   Your character, a divorced father, takes his son on a vacation to Israel. They're standing at a booth in a bazaar. One moment the boy is beside him. The next moment he has vanished without a sound.

☞   Someone picks your character's pocket in Gibraltar. He grabs her wallet and passport and sells it to someone who assumes her identity.

☞   After a very stressful career, your character's husband retires. He was an experienced business traveler, but she had never been out of the country. They fly to Prague for a vacation. He has a heart attack and dies in the baggage claim area.

☞   When your character returns from Hong Kong, he tells the customs officer, "Nothing to declare." They do a strip search and find the watch, the diamond earrings, the gold lighter, the jade pendant, and the label in his tailor-made suit.

☞   As she and her husband walked up the gangplank to the ship, your character gasps. She recognized the cruise director. Five years ago, she had had a wild, passionate, secretive affair with him on a vacation to Ibiza.

☞   Passengers pushed and shoved in the crowded boarding area. Under the circumstances, your character didn't see or feel anything unusual. The airport dogs sniffed out the cocaine in her carry-on bag.

☞   The third day of the race, a storm moved in, breaking the mast. For the next three suspenseful days, your character,

the skipper, learned more than he had ever wanted to
know about his crew.

☞ Your character cashed in her stock portfolio and went on
a cruise to find a husband.

☞ Your character takes a vacation to the mountains. On a
whim he buys a log cabin and stays.

☞ Your character had moved uptown when he became successful. It was the longest and hardest trip he had ever
taken. After his concerts, he went back downtown to the
jazz clubs to sit in. It made him feel clean. His wife said
money did not make her feel dirty.

☞ Your character, a Detroit architect and a bachelor, is sent
to Atlanta by his firm on a project that goes on for months.
He meets a young woman so Southern he describes her to
friends back home as honey batter dipped and deep fried.
When his work is over, they get married and go back to
Detroit. What had seemed charming in Atlanta began to
seem pretentious and defensive. The more he cooled, the
more she turned on what she considered her "moonlight
on the magnolias" charms . . . or you could choose for
her to be a sympathetic protagonist. Your call.

CHAPTER 16

Food

After Tina Brown became the editor of *The New Yorker* and had the audacity to make some changes to the city's flagship magazine, many loyal subscribers have not stopped grousing. I forgave her for all her sins, however, when she began to publish Special Fiction Issues. But I must admit to muttering when a recent one opened with an article explaining, or defending, why they had asked a number of authors to write about food. Food indeed. You don't put a pork chop in a poem. You fry it with a slice of apple. For my taste, the staffer, Bill Buford, made too many cute puns on fiction being nourishing. But I began to be interested when he said stories originate in memory, and storytellers asked to muse about food came back with tales prompted by the memories and associations that food had evoked for them.

First there was Salman Rushdie's "Leavened Bread," an account of having grown up on chapati and phulka and his feeling disloyal when he fell gluttonously in love with the "plentiful promiscuity" of English leavened bread he bought "in the whorehouse of the bakeries." Okay, so his essay was about emigration, not bread, but I still wasn't completely sold on this idea of food being the theme for the fiction issue.

I stopped crabbing, however, when I read Elizabeth Hardwick's "Grits Soufflé." Even she admitted using the word grits with souffle was "like putting a hat on a donkey," but Hardwick can always be trusted with language. She has an educated palate:

"Grits, groats, grout, gruel are Old English words of a granite beauty, strength, and resonance. They tell of hard times, of rural folk, and of orphans starved by fat caretakers in Dickens." But then she compared a grits soufflé to the pomp and puff of a defiant marriage—her soufflé triggering my memory of her and Robert Lowell, to the extent I couldn't concentrate on my own work for the rest of the day. In my imagination, Lowell and Hardwick sit next to Brontë's romantic fictional lovers Cathy and Heathcliff.

My admiration for Hardwick's work knows no bounds, and as long as she was married to a great poet, I felt there was order in the universe. When he left her for Caroline Blackwood, whom I refused to think of as "Lady" anything, I wanted revenge. Then Lowell published *For Lizzie and Harriet* (Hardwick and their daughter). I thought, aha, he regrets. But what really fed my quixotic fantasy was his death from a heart attack. He was in a cab on his way from the airport to Hardwick's apartment. Oh, I have Ian Hamilton's biography of Lowell on my bookshelf, but I don't want to read about the poet's drinking problems and his bouts with depression or the possibility of his having had a practical reason—like delivering an alimony check—for going to Hardwick's apartment the day he died. I dislike reading stories about people's lives when you already know how the tale turns out. I would rather imagine if Lowell and Hardwick had been reunited, they would have served as each other's muse, creating their best work to inspire the ages . . . and thanks to her soufflé, for the rest of the day I did.

Maybe Buford was on to something. . . .

Gooseberry pie, my favorite kind, symbolizes loss. The bushes have lots of nasty stickers. Nobody picks the ber-

ries anymore. The bushes and the women who used to
gather the berries and make the pies for me rather than
birthday cakes are gone. Birthdays have lost their punch.
Who wants to celebrate with a cake from Sara Lee, for pity
sakes. When my mother died, one of the ladies from the
church apologized when she delivered the last gooseberry
pie I have ever tasted. The berries were canned. At ninety
years old, she couldn't pick anymore, but she had been
saving this last jar. She'd made the pie special with lots
of sugar.

Action, facts, dialogue, put flesh on a character's skeleton, but symbolic association can offer the deepest sense
of him. Let's say you create a tycoon who has made a fortune as a ship builder. Facts: He is seventy years old,
slightly stooped, but lean as a greyhound and shrewd as
a lynx. In his luxurious town house, there is a butler's
pantry with many shelves filled with tins of sliced peaches.
Each night he has the peaches for dessert, even insists
they be served at his otherwise elegant dinner parties. He
was a child of the Depression, always hungry. There is a
symbolic story about the tins of peaches.

Try telling a Jewish mother chicken soup isn't symbolic.

We express our love and celebrate our rituals with traditional edibles like birthday cakes with candles, candy
shaped like hearts, chocolate bunny rabbits, and eggs
painted gay colors. Perish the thought of an American
Thanksgiving without a turkey and stuffing, even for those,
like me, who rank the taste of the bird just above card-
board, but a tad below cauliflower. Vary a conventional
holiday menu and prepare to endure family disappointment, if not suffer scorn. However, if you have created a
character you intend to develop as a rebel, an outsider, or
an eccentric, show it without telling by having her expect
her guests to give a blessing when she serves vegetarian
spaghetti, an anchovy pizza, stuffed cabbage, or Chinese
takeout for the Thanksgiving feast.

Food contributes to defining a country's culture, especially Christmas eating customs. John Lanchester's *New
Yorker* essay "Plum Pudding" gives the recipe for the con-
coction, but it reveals more about British nationalism and
expatriotism. In the background, I heard echoes of an E.M.
Forster novel set in a time when there still was an Empire:

Lanchester ate his first seventeen Christmas puddings in the Far East, primarily Hong Kong, where the thermometer usually registered in the seventies. Not the ideal weather, he admits, for a feast conceived to be consumed in the winter far to the north. He is convinced the Cantonese must have thought they were mad and thinks perhaps they were right. Much of the family's expatriate colonial life was an attempt to live as if Hong Kong were actually a district in England.

The Lanchesters' Christmas pudding, their entire culture, he believes was a defense against the strangeness of where they were. "The predictable result was that a meal intended to celebrate a traditional Christmas (in an England I scarcely knew) now infallibly and overpoweringly reminds me of Hong Kong. The taste it leaves is oddly dark, even bitter."

We attach figurative significance to food, because we, like Lanchester, make sense of our lives through our senses. Historically, writers have added reality to their stories by metaphorically evoking tastes and smells associated with our experiences. In another short *New Yorker* piece called "Indigestion," Anton Chekhov describes Podtikin's waiting for, preparing, and starting to eat his sumptuous blini. Although he so vividly describes the rich food and drink, a reader can get heartburn from the language, it is Podtikin's gluttony which makes the most striking impression.

FIGURATIVE LANGUAGE

Figures of speech or poetic language, like Rushdie's "whorehouses of bakeries," depart from standard construction, order, and significance of words to achieve special meaning or consequence. Effective figures of speech surprise us with the unlikeness of two things compared, while at the same time convincing us of the aptness or truth of the likeness. To extend his metaphor and I assume to amuse himself, Rushdie uses hyperbole to describe the English yeast bread:

"The soft, pillowy mattressiness of it. The well-sprung bounciness of it between your teeth."

Note the impressive way Chekhov uses poetic language in "Indigestion" to describe the setting, develop his character, and render a "not what you expect" but credible conclusion. He appeals to our mouths and our eyes with his description of the blini, "crisp, lacy and plump as the shoulders of a merchant's daughter." Podtikin douses it in butter, caviar, sour cream, a sprat, a sardine, and the "oiliest" slice of salmon. While he waits for his feast he looks at the liquor lined up on the table as if he were a general surveying a battlefield and the bottles were lined up by rank. Impatiently watching the preparation of the food, "his eyes melted like butter; his face oozed with lust."

The writer built the suspense until we the readers were greedily waiting for our taste. Then when we and Podtikin can wait no longer, gasping and trembling with pleasure, and smacking his lips, he prepared the blini, drank a shot of vodka, ". . . opened his mouth—and was struck by an apoplectic fit."

Chekhov liberally spiced his piece with similes, comparisons that use "like" or "as"—"his eyes melted like butter." A metaphor implies the comparison—"his face oozed with lust."

Our common speech patterns contain poetic language used so often we don't think of the figurative significance. For example, when we use the metaphor, "the eye of the potato," we don't mean to suggest the potato can actually see. We simply mean the leafbud looks like an eye. However, if you wanted to show your character's anger at her husband as she worked in the kitchen, you could have her gouge out the eye of a potato rather than simply peel it, implying that she is symbolically gouging out her husband's eyes. In this case, the strong verb empowers a cliché.

If you have written a story about a financial type who is telling his client news of a merger that is about to break, you might have him tell it metaphorically: "This hot potato comes out of the oven on Wednesday."

Wilted lettuce is an edible oxymoron, as is sweet and sour pork. A paradoxical statement that combines two terms that in ordinary usage are contraries can be effective. Look at "friendly fire." Fire from a hip you know isn't friendly; it hurts even worse. Imagine a story about two brothers hunting. One accidentally shoots the other. Patsy Cline not only became famous after she recorded "Honky Tonk Angel," but the oxymoron helped to define her paradoxical character. Martha Graham, another artist with conflicting characteristics, has been called a Sacred Monster.

If you enjoy playing around with words, puns are as irresistible chocolate-covered cherries, but go easy. When the language in your story begins to call attention to itself, you're in trouble. Your cleverness detracts from your story. My recent favorite is the possibly apocryphal story about the Japanese tourist who goes into a bookstore and asks for the title *Angry Raisins.* The clerk finally determines what he wants is *The Grapes of Wrath.* A company looking for web programmers ran this ad: "Desperately Seeking Surfers."

In her piece about the soufflé, Hardwick's use of alliteration, "Grits, groats, grout, gruel are Old English words of a granite beauty," added a poetic flavor to her dish, but she only employed the figure of speech once. Stuffing without sage would be as bland as bones, but too much makes it bite like a bulldog. I can hardly resist alliteration, even when it stretches logic, perhaps that is why I've been blessed with a list of students' names that help to satiate my urge. At the moment there is: Jim, Jess, Jeremy, John, and Jane.

The same rule—less is best—works when adding figures of speech to your stories.

As poets attribute magic to the stars, in Chang-rae Lee's *New Yorker* essay, "Beans," he gives the mystical power to beans, stopping just short of personifying (endowing an inanimate object with human attributes) them as soldiers. But, married to an Italian, he does say they are the true "heart of the Italian kitchen" and suggests when cooking, their sweet smell takes him "through a door of the past" where the inglorious legume has been known to save lives.

A chef could be transformed into a poet if he listened to what his food and utensils were saying. Fast frying bacon "crackles," corn "pops," tea kettles "hiss" and "splutter," sinks "gurgle." Turn a pancake and listen to it "flop" and "plop." Maybe it was a cook with good ears who started calling them flapjacks. Pans "clack" against each other.

Words created to imitate the sound they make are examples of onomatopoeia and can help to add a sound track to your work. You could give a clearer picture of a character who murmurs, mumbles, grumbles, whispers than of one who just talks. Bells tinkle, hens and overly protective mothers cluck over their wayward children who whoop. Onomatopoeia can add a buzz to a boring line.

The following test Bill Burford's theory that food can satisfy your appetite for a tasty story to tell:

STORY STARTERS

☞   Your character and her husband had gone out for burritos when her labor for their only child started early. Every time she saw them on a menu she remembered that night—the last time they had ever done anything as a team.

☞   Your character, a romantic, put the engagement ring he had bought for the more pragmatic Joan in the chocolate mousse. She swallowed it.

☞   Your character receives a Fulbright scholarship to study in Korea. He falls in love with and marries a young woman from Seoul. The story takes place at the first Seder she prepares for his Orthodox family when the couple return to New York.

☞   Your character owns and operates a seafood restaurant on a wharf in Maine. She makes elaborate excuses why she always has the help boil the lobsters. Actually she thinks the practice is cruel and inhumane. She begins to have hideous dreams that don't go away with the dawn.

☞   Your character's father, a salesman, traveled and never could make it to baseball games, Boy Scout outings, etc. But Mr. Benson, a next-door neighbor, whom the kids called Benny, always took your character to all the Cardinal home games. They made a big day out of it, had hot dogs with all the trimmings at the park for lunch, and sometimes got a player's autograph. When your character grew up, every time he smelled hot dogs, he missed—not Benny—but his father.

☞   When the scale registered 225 pounds, your character went to Weight Watchers and joined an exercise program.

One entire wall of the workout room was mirrored. As she huffed and puffed, she could not miss seeing her huge jiggling stomach or the tree-trunk-sized thighs. She did not hate herself, however. She hated her mother, the good cook, who showed her love through deep-dish apple pies bubbling with sugar and spices, larded pork roasts sizzling with golden brown crackling crusts of sage and rosemary, plump onions floating in a sea of cream and butter.

☞ Your character was born on the Iowa farm his family had owned and operated for three generations. When he was ten, he watched his father and brother butcher a pig. That was the day he became a vegetarian. He tells the story in flashbacks from medical school, where he has just begun his surgery rotation and has experienced a disturbing epiphany.

☞ Your character, the chairman of a medium-sized pharmaceutical company, did not become the skipper by being a pansy. In the midst of eighteen-hour days of tough negotiations for a merger that will make her the chief operating officer of the combined companies, they break for lunch in the executive dining room. Your character, called behind her back the Iron Lady, absently takes a bite of the dessert set in front of her. She jerks, drops her eyes to the dish in front of her, stares at it, then suddenly begins to cry as she dashes from the table. It is a bowl of baked custard, something she had not tasted nor thought about for years, not since she deserted her husband and child, who had insisted upon Mommy's making baked custard for her every single day.

☞ Your character, married to a prominent physician, calls it the curse of conformity, but she tongues the medicine he gives her when she is ill. After he has gone to the office, she reaches for a jar of honey, slices a lemon, opens the fifth of Irish whiskey, and prepares her mother's cure, the only thing that ever makes her well.

☞ The doctor thought the mayonnaise in the chicken salad might have gone rancid in the heat. What else would explain why everyone at the garden wedding—including the bride and groom—had ended the festivities in the emergency room?

☞ Your character remembers the Fourth of July picnic when she was eight. Her mother and her aunt have not spoken since that day—the one when she accidentally sat down on her aunt's coconut-cream pie in her new pale blue dress.

☞ After the divorce, your character thought the night her in-laws came for dinner and she made the popovers that didn't pop had been the beginning of the end.

☞ To raise money for the Sunday School, your character's church had sponsored an old-fashioned pie supper. Your character baked a cherry pie, tied it up in a red-and-white checked tea towel and went to the event with Charles, whom she had been seeing for over a year. For a reason she was not to know, Charles's best friend John bid against him for her pie, paying a ridiculous price to buy it. After the sale, the men went outside and had a fight. Then they both stalked off without saying a word to her. The story is about her finally learning, after years have passed, what prompted the incident.

☞ Red Jell-o and hospitals were synonyms for your character. At a class reunion luncheon, the waitress sets a red Jell-o salad in front of her and she begins to weep.

☞ Your character associated people with food. Sugar cookies made her think of her grandmother. Uncle Jay always smelled like garlic. Pot roast reminded her of her husband, but caviar was reserved for Eric, whom she wished she had married.

☞ Your character married a handsome ne'er-do-well who fancied himself a poet. One of the ways she had supported them was renting a pizza parlor's oven after they closed to bake muffins and cookies that she sold door to door. People loved her baking. Finally, a local banker, whose wife bought her muffins, suggested the bank loan her money to open a bakery and a restaurant. It was successful. Now she had money, and she still had the handsome, ne'er-do-well husband. How success affects both of them is the story. (Think ''not what you expect.'')

CHAPTER 17

Clothes That Make the Story

The image of the scarlet letter on Hester Prynne's plain Puritan dress has lasted as if it were seared on our brains with a red-hot branding iron. Fitzgerald flappers still loll about in floaty white dresses when they aren't dancing the Charleston. Holden Caulfield's red hunting cap might have started the trend for kids wearing the bills of ball caps at rakish angles, but book illustrators have made more of Huck's straw hat than Twain did. Except in mysteries, what characters wear usually has little significance unless they serve as symbols like the scarlet letter or reveal character like Holden's cap. Tolstoy dressed Anna Karenina in elegant gowns and furs, but who remembers what she was wearing when she threw herself in front of the train?

Clothes can be clues when there is a crime to solve—blood stains on the glove, a bullet hole in a sleeve, the victim remembering her attacker's Hawaiian shirt. The accused Grace Marks, Margaret Atwood's protagonist in *Alias Grace*, wears the murder victim's pretty clothes to the trial.

Grace's vain decision is threaded through the plot like a red ribbon. It raises doubt about her version of the story, reveals an admirable aspect of this poor girl's tidy character, offers motivation for the prosecution's attempt to hang her.

The decision for you, the writer, to make is this: What do I accomplish if I put my character in a blue dress with puffed sleeves, a full skirt cinched at the waist with a turquoise belt? Does it matter if it's blue, black, or purple? Why does the reader need to know the color of her dress or even if she's wearing a dress, suit, or jeans? You use language as carefully and economically as your paycheck. If you spend words and space describing the man's rumpled suit, the button missing on her bodice, the number of earrings they wear in their ears, it has to have some value. The reader expects for the details to mean something.

However, clothes can also start a story. Like food, memories attach themsleves to what we wore, where we wore them, why we bought them, what they symbolized.

I see a closet. At the back, there is a fat blue plastic bag covering an elegant silk wedding dress with inserts of fine Madeira lace. The forty-foot train has been folded many times to fit under the protective cover. The gossamer veil flows from a crown of seed pearls. The dress has been there for a long time. It has never been worn. What's the story?

I see another beautiful wedding dress. It has a minute stain over the heart, perhaps blood from a pin prick. Your character's soon-to-be mother-in-law suggests it would be wasteful for her to buy another when this is just her size and so lovely. The dress belonged to your character's fiancé's first wife—the one who was killed two months after the wedding, the one whose portrait still hangs next to his on his mother's wall.

I see a closet with a locked door. Your character discovers it is locked when she spends the night in her soon-to-be husband's apartment. He has been called into the office for a few hours and can't drive her home to pick up her casual clothes. Rather than spending the morning in the party dress from the night before, she is hoping to wear one of his shirts. After a search, she finds the key to open Pandora's box. Do the slinky, silk nightgowns, satin negligees, high-heeled mules belong to another woman, a large woman . . . or are they for his pleasure?

I see a closet neatly divided between the black clothes and the suits, pants, dresses, and sweaters in bright splashy—even gaudy—colors. The hook on the bathroom door holds two robes: one made from heavy black terry cloth; the other from a slick, shiny fabric, orange as a tangerine. Your character, who suffers from manic depression, dresses to express her moods. When her husband and twin sons still lived here, they watched cautiously to see which robe she wore to breakfast. They meant well, but poor dears, they could never understand the gravity of her mission. The messages, sent to her from beyond, were zoomed into her closet. Her clothes held the secrets that would purify the universe. God knows she had tried to explain to them her responsibility and to include them in her tasks, like breaking all the television screens with a hammer, but even when she put the boys in the closet and locked the door, they couldn't hear the instructions. It was just as well that they were gone.

When your character is packing, he finds a box with his tuxedo stored carefully in it. Lovingly, he unfolds the tissue bearing the name of the fashionable London shop where it had been tailored to his measure. Now the shirt with the pleated front looked as if it had been dipped in egg yolk, but he could remember when it had been as sparkling white and pristine as a christening robe. It could probably be bleached out. No studs. They had been pawned some time ago, but one didn't have to have solid gold. He slips into the jacket, a little large now, but after he put on a few pounds it would look swell again. He runs his hand down the sleeve . . . what? Moths. Sneaky pests. The lousy coat was riddled with so many holes, it looked as if someone had used it for target practice. Taking off the jacket and throwing it in the black garbage bag with the rest of the trash, your character smiles cynically and thinks maybe someone had.

Your character takes his seven-year-old son to a toy shop to buy a costume for his second-grade Halloween party. The boy wants to be a space raider. As his father shuffles the hangers looking for the right size, he comes to a clown suit. He remembers a Halloween thirty-five years ago, when his mother had sat up late at night sewing bright-colored, puffy balls on a clown suit for him that he had refused to wear. That was the year his father had walked out on them. He had insisted upon going as a ghost. Thirty-five years ago every boy had had a dad.

To make any of the previous stories interesting, you must take the reader to the scene, let her see where she is, whom she is with, what is happening. For as long as it takes to read your tale, she must disappear into the world that you, the magician, have created for her.

DESCRIPTION THAT DOESN'T STOP THE ACTION

When someone decides to read a story, she has made an agreement with the author to suspend disbelief. Even though at the end of the day, she is snuggled into a chenille robe in a comfortable reading chair in her study, which sits on a two-acre lot in Toledo, the reader will allow herself the illusion of riding on a double-decker bus down London's King's Road early in he morning on a drizzly day, as long as the writer keeps his part of the bargain and does not remind her she is only reading a fictional account of that bus trip.

Let's pretend the story has a naive narrator, Charlie, a genuine innocent aboard, who hadn't been particularly savvy about how the world worked in the small town in Iowa where he lived, and who is now getting it all wrong in London. Dickens would have said he lived in Hicksville, but I consider that telling not showing. (Dickens, like the framers of the Bible, got away with breaking most of the writing rules that I cherish. Trying to determine why is another book.)

One way to show Charlie's ineptness would be to dress him funny. His clothes could be out of date, inappropriate, or simply in deplorable taste. But we have him on the bus, and two women of the night on their way home from working Piccadilly Circus have just climbed aboard and are looking him over. If we stop to say: Charlie is wearing a green-and-yellow plaid jacket. His tie has a hand-painted orange tractor in the center. His boots have thick white rubber soles, then we have slammed the brakes on the action. We've sent a message to the reader—hold that thought while I describe what my character is wearing. The illusion of being on that bus with some poor guy who might be on the edge of trouble is destroyed.

You can describe through dialogue: "Hey, mate, where'd you get that neat tie you're wearing?" the blond lady in the skimpiest skirt Charlie had ever seen in his life asked. "Why, thank you kindly. My implement dealer back home in Iowa gave it to me when I bought my new tractor. See it's orange, just like the one I drive."

Another way is go into a character's thoughts: Charlie couldn't make head nor tails of these English folks like that friendly lady smiling at him from across the aisle. Here she was early in the morning, all rigged out for a grand party in black lace socks, little white boots, and a red satin blouse that, to be honest, was so tight it showed her nipples.

Try to use similar techniques when depicting a setting or giving a physical description of a character. Rather than saying it was raining, have your character feel the water running down the neck of her coat or be unable to see through the windshield of her jeep. It's more effective to have a man stand on his tiptoes to see in the small window in the front door of his house than to say he is short.

When describing clothes, choose things for your character to wear that tell more. If your character happens to be the editor of a fashion magazine, what she wears and why she makes the choice could be essential to the plot. If a divorced father wears cowboy boots to his daughter's very formal wedding only to irritate or get the attention of his former wife, the boots reveal character and arouse curiosity. If she is married to someone else, but your character is not and he wants her back, the reader will be eager to know what happens.

Since we often make snap judgments about people simply from what they are wearing, devious people can use clothes to cover up more than their naked bodies. There is the legendary Mafia boss who for years has wondered around New York streets in his bathrobe pretending to be mad. There are those who say selling that story is the cleverest job he has ever pulled.

The crooks, who for a year robbed many of the most exclusive shops on Madison Avenue, were among the best-dressed men in town. They didn't break locks or windows, they rang the bell. Proprietors saw the Armani suits and buzzed them in.

Recently, many successful robbers have worn UPS uniforms. I once met a woman from an affluent Chicago suburb who said after the neighbors left on vacation, she was out in the yard when two men in white coveralls came out of the neighbors' house carrying their Oriental carpets. While they were putting them in their white panel truck, she said, "Oh, would you mind taking mine, too? I've been meaning to call someone to clean them." They said they would be happy to oblige her. Neither she nor her neighbor ever saw their expensive rugs again.

I think there is an ironic story in a "clothes make the man" tale.

Clothes, like food, help to define rituals like christening robes and a boy's first suit and tie. Usually, you will find stories stored away with them in trunks, cedar chests, and the mind's attic where memories are stashed.

STORY STARTERS

☞ Your character, an ambitious sixteen-year-old, finally landed her first runway modeling job. They handed her a sheer, totally see-through evening dress. In all the confusion backstage, no one noticed she didn't wear a body suit, or an opaque underslip.

☞ Your character had been wearing a sea-tinted evening dress with a handkerchief hem. The set was a beach with seagulls shrilling on a sound track. The shot was set for the couple to meet and embrace. By the time they had done many takes, she was sure she loved the handsome young man whose name she didn't know. Foolishly, she had bought the sea-tinted dress, had the ad framed on her bedroom wall. She had never worked with him again.

☞ On a whim your character bought a gorgeous white evening dress with pearls stitched into glorious designs. It was too luxurious to wear. She hung it like a painting to remember a perfect day she had spent diving in the Southern Grenadines between Grenada and St. Vincent. They had done shallow dives in water brilliant with colors she'd never seen before, had stood under fresh inland water falls, and in the afternoon had stopped at a beach with black sand where they had dived for sand dollars and floated on their backs eating the tamarinds and coconuts they'd picked themselves. On the way back, she had sat on the bow of the boat and a pod of sixty dolphins appeared to escort them home. There hadn't been a perfect day since.

☞ In the dim glow of a night-light, the father sat by the hospital bed where his son fought for life. He hadn't seen him for five years. When the boy's mother called, she had said the trouble had all started over the leather jacket he had mailed the boy for his birthday.

☞ Their pictures appeared regularly on the society pages. Your character's husband was so often asked to chair, or at least allow them to use his name, at the fund-raising galas. She had one entire closet filled with evening gowns bearing designer labels. Now this perspiring Saks Fifth Avenue store detective was trying to make her tell him why she had shoplifted a thirty-five-dollar French barrette. He had a long wait in store. She planned never to tell anyone.

☞ To anyone else, it was simply a uniform. To your character, it was a disguise. Every day your character could put it on and cover up that other undesirable person.

☞ Your character collects hats. They are her diary. Each one represents a phase of her life, an important event, a trip. Friends and family beg for the stories. She tells about all but one. That is her secret.

☞ When your character is preparing to move to a new town, she buys a wardrobe of maternity clothes and a pregnancy pillow like actresses use in movies and on the stage.

☞ In a cleaning flurry, your character attacks the attic. Everything is covered with dust except her husband's army foot locker, which had a higher polish than her kitchen floor. She opened the lid, wondering why he had been up here messing around with this old stuff. Folded neatly on top of his sergeant's uniform she found a baby's jacket . . . a baby's jacket like she had seen only in pictures. It was made from a quilted Oriental fabric.

☞ Your character's husband had bought her many bathrobes, but she always returned them and continued to wear the ratty old terry cloth with holes in both sleeves. Once it had been emerald green. The color had mostly washed out, but not the stains. She told her husband it had belonged to her father and held sentimental value. It was only a partial lie. It did have sentimental value, but it hadn't belonged to her father. That was all Alex, the love of her life, had left when he moved out.

☞ Your character was amazed when her eighteen-year-old daughter wanted to participate in the debutante season. "Being a deb is back," the daughter explained, and began to ask her mother to go with her to fittings at Vera Wang and Bergdorf Goodman, sittings for Bachrach portraits. They brought her father into the plans when they had to line up escorts for the balls. The story is about your character's taking out her sleeveless white dress and long kid gloves—the ones she wore to her International Debutante Ball. She had packed away a secret with the dress, one she had never told anyone, especially her husband, John, who in 1966 had been in love with Liz Sloan, her classmate at Smith. Your character's and John's parents—prominent families with newsworthy names—had always been friends. She and John were friends, but he had not returned her love. When she had told Liz she was going to ask John to be her escort for her deb ball, Liz had said it was a test. If he did, she would never see him again. His parents had forced him to accept. The media had made a big to-do, Liz had dumped him, she and John eventually drifted into marriage. He still pined for Liz Sloan. Her daughter would also be coming out.

CHAPTER 18

Words

If you have diligently read the previous chapters, with the exception of the climax and conclusion—appropriately saved for the final chapter—you now have contemplated a list of the essential ingredients for a story: a fully developed character, conflict, suspense and tension, and effective point of view, a recognizable voice and appropriate tone, the cause and effect of incidents creating the complications, a sense of time and place, descriptive details to create images. In the passage to follow, you will have an opportunity to consider how to build your plot to a climax that changes the situation or the character and leads your story to a fitting end. But here is the moment of truth.

Literature is all about language. Unfortunately, you can master the techniques, build in all of the proper elements, and still turn out a story as flat, dull, and tasteless as one of Hardwick's soufflés that doesn't puff. Substitute "raise" for "puff" in her essay and, if you have a writer's soul, you will mourn the loss. If words don't fascinate you, make you giggle, make you cry, make your heart pound faster, do yourself a favor and take up snowboarding. Without a passion for the magic of words, writing is just work.

You can't buy a writer's soul at Saks or have one made to order. Unless it is a gift from the gods, I do not know where it comes from, but I do know it when I hear it and see it at work. The fact the roof still sits squarely on the New School always amazes me. On a few rare and wondrous occasions, I have heard a voice so fresh, so original, and so powerful, I've felt the building move on its foundation, like the day "Andy" Burgess read a passage from his almost completed novel, *Cowards.*

Perceptive but stoned, Mitch Slaughter—the protagonist—grabbed me by the throat and the heart, dragging me into a world I did not want to see or believe really existed except in the hyped imaginations of voyeurist journalists filing shocking stories from the Seattle scene. The heroin-haunted language, the sometimes brutal, sometimes ridiculous vistas of Mitch and the drugged-out-of-mind members of his rock band, horrified and magnetized. I wanted to save him.

Listening that day in class, my mind did paradoxical dips—soaring to the rhythm of the art—crashing to the imagined beat of commercial publishing. This wasn't a tacky "the way we wish it were" romance, an "I'm so glad it's not happening to me" horror, or yet another "whodunit movie disguised as a novel." Where was the Maxwell Perkins who developed Fitzgerald, Hemingway, and Wolfe? I was so afraid no editor would be brave enough to take a chance with this unique but unknown voice. Oh, ye of little faith . . .

As I complete this manuscript, a galley from St. Martin's Press lies on my desk absorbing the light. The flap copy begins: "Occasionally a great writer comes out of nowhere to tell his generation's story. With his first novel W.A. Burgess has arrived."

Out of the scores who have passed through the New School classes and the Maine workshops, there are a few other originals like Andy. If luck's a lady, they, too, will connect with a courageous editor. Maybe you will find an idea in this book to start a story that will speak to you in a voice as fresh as a new day. I hope so. Writing is not a competitive sport. Those of us who profess to teach it, and are honest, know two things: We are apt to meet those who will be able to write the way we only wish we could, and writing cannot be taught. At best we can encourage, support, and be another set of more objective eyes and ears to hear clunkers, recognize a digression, need to know more about a character, see a plot hole.

However, I agreed with Anne Lamo when she said in *bird by bird* that publishing is not what it's cracked up to be, but writing is. You will feel the pleasure at those moments when language does magic tricks. It happens often in the workshops I teach like when Frankie, Paul's young protagonist, describes cutting his grandfather's disgusting toenails and it brings tears to your eyes, or you want to shake Haley's Billy as he touches the snake in front of the church congregation and thinks he has been anointed. When Jim created the good/bad girl Sage, but killed her off after one chapter, I felt I should go to her funeral. But I fear I'll never be able to shake a sacrilegious view of weddings and funerals after looking from the ironic viewpoint of Hugh's Celeste, an organist performing musical tricks to cover up the faux pas behind her.

I know Frankie, Sage, Celeste, and company better than I know most of my New York neighbors. Tell me that's not magic.

If there is a reader's disease like alcoholism, thankfully, I have it. Unfortunately, I have a lazy memory, but out of the thousands of books I've read, a few authors have written lines that hit me so hard, I'm imprinted for life. If you want to make a success of writing, your goal should be to find the terms to express a truth, to show beauty, to surprise, to shock, to change perspective, in a way that your reader will never forget. Here are a few of the lines that have made a lasting impression on me:

In Horatio's farewell speech to Hamlet, he says: "Now cracks a noble heart. Good night,/sweet Prince,/And flights of angels sing thee to they rest."

If I were to be marooned on a desert island and could only take one poem, apologetically, it would not be one by Shelley, Dickinson, Hopkins, Auden, those whose work I also admire. It would be "The Love Song of J. Alfred Prufrock." The fun begins with the paradoxical title, which reminds me of my father, who died with "I love you" still stuck in his throat, but he used to buy the mushiest valentines Hallmark made for Mother, my sister, me, and sign them all: W.T. Willett.

Prufrock plays with words the way I hope you will. I've read his interior monologue a trillion times and he still makes me laugh, cry, and say "Eureka." Eliot, who seems to have been as stiff as a mechanized cadaver, was much too guarded to have allowed anyone to know he entertained such indecorous ideas. He never enters my mind. The poet has created a character and a voice so authentic, he has written himself out of the narrative, and thankfully doesn't intrude. The thoughts are Prufrock's. Of course, that's the second joke. The poem opens with a quote by a spirit from Dante's *Inferno* who says he would never speak if anyone could ever hear his words, but no one returns from hell. In this case, hell is Prufrock's mind. The reader is asked to suspend disbelief and to imagine she is only listening in on confessional musings. Prufrock, who has measured out his life in coffee spoons, who worries about his thinning hair and waning sexual potency, is much too proper, vain, and self-conscious to utter such revealing concerns aloud.

Three novels have knocked the breath out of me with one short sentence, in one case, a single word. After spending pages and pages in *Heart of Darkness* with Conrad's Kurtz, I gasped, but understood the power of the darkness when he said, "Exterminate all the brutes."

Every year for at least the last twenty, I have reread Hardy's *Jude the Obscure,* in hopes this time things will turn out better, but the line is always still there. His small son still hangs his siblings and himself. "Done because we are too menney."

In Tim Winton's *The Riders,* Fred Scully's tough seven-year-old daughter, Billie, loyally accompanies her father on a love-crazed odyssey in search of her mother, who has vanished. When the wandering is about to destroy them both, finally, the wise child simply says, "Me," and Scully realizes he must indeed choose his daughter and give up the obsessive dark journey.

I can no longer find the context for Elizabeth Hardwick's understated line that made me sign on as a fan for life.

The incident occurred soon after Robert Lowell absconded, and the media made much of her as the abandoned wife. A friend, who might have meant well, asked her if she was terribly lonely. "Not always," she said.

Through the years, my gallant sister has mailed most of my wardrobe back to me piece by piece—things I've misplaced, forgotten when packing after a visit. (I chose "gallant" to imply courteous. It was more economical than writing another sentence: "She does this troublesome task without complaining or preaching to me.") My Dunhill lighter has spent almost as much time in some post office as in my cigarette case. I constantly lose my glasses, my gloves. I have even lost my laptop computer a couple of time, but misplacing a passage like Hardwick's "not always" or a word is what really frustrates me.

Recently, Keith—one of the writers in my workshop—thought I had gone daft as I became ecstatic when she (Keith is a woman; her parents were expecting a boy) used "doppelgänger" (a ghostly double of a living person, especially one that haunts its own fleshly counterpart) in her story. It was one of my lost words, gone for so long. I like the tongue-twister sound and it has an entire story built into its meaning. I am so glad to have it back.

Then working on this manuscript I fond "anthropomorphism" (the attributing of human characteristics to gods, animals, and objects). It is a bit of a show-off word, but more apt to grab the attention of someone who has slipped into the practice unaware, like calling herself "Mommie" to a scruffy cat, for pity sakes.

For weeks, I had been searching in my mind's Lost and Found for the word used when someone lends his name to something like the title of a book, restaurant, company. I assumed it would turn up eventually, most likely in an article about Donald Trump, who has a proclivity for naming everything after himself, but in the meantime I was forced to waste a dozen words when one would have done. I should have immediately called Ellen, my friend and former editor. She works crossword puzzles. Ellen even knew how to spell "eponymous." My computer's spell check does not, and its thesaurus has never even heard of the word. My friend should create computer software. She could call it something like "Ellen's Elusive Word Bank."

Some words get lost because they lose their luster and go out of fashion. I usually like reduplication words—those that repeat themselves with little or no change, but if you have a character say "hubba hubba," be sure he's a World War II veteran with a case of arrested development. No one really knows the origin, but it was a sign of enthusiasm, usually over the anatomy of a woman wearing rationed shoes, and something a squad of forties soldiers said automatically when given the command, "At ease."

Some reduplication, still a part of the vernacular that, used sparingly, might add a little zip-and-zing to your story are:

shilly-shally	fiddle-faddle
spic-and-span	mishmash
willy-nilly	huggermugger
hurly-burly	hurdy-gurdy
dingdong	pooh-pooh
rooty-tooty	dipsy-doodle
boogie-woogie	

After you have worked like a dog," "burned the midnight oil," if you don't want to "bite the dust," but have your story "sell like hotcakes," you might as well "face the music" and "quick as a wink" remove all clichés, the "fatal flaw" of writing. Clichés suck the vitality right out of your work, leaving it as dry and unappetizing as turkey warmed over the sixth day after Thanksgiving. Here's the test: If you think of a word like "dawn," "facts," "daylight," and a phrase comes to mind such as: "crack of dawn," "facts of life," "broad daylight," it is probably a cliché. To use fresh language, it isn't necessary to invent new words like James Joyce, just avoid the overfamiliar like a cloud with a "silver lining" and a "skeleton in a closet."

It would be irresponsible to close without a reminder about the potency of verbs. Don't scurry through your story, settling for the first fitting action word. Imagine a scene where one of your characters is going to strike another. Think "cause and effect." What kind of emotional response do you desire from your reader? Do you want her to wince, or be horrified, or are the consequences not to be severe?

If two brothers have a tiff that will be forgotten in an hour, you won't pick a word with the connotative power you will need to show the cruelty of a criminal attacking a victim. All of the following mean to strike someone or something, but note the difference in impact:

pummel	pound	slug
cudgel	trounce	pound
thrash	spank	whip
flog	flagellate	flail
batter	beat	hit
clobber	scourge	slap

"Ayo, listen up." "The nine-one-one" on using slang in your story is this: The phrase you use might have gone out of style before the ink dries on your paper, and that's "the inside skinny." As we go to press, thanks to rap lyrics, hip-hop is shoving Valley Girl talk into obsolescence but "gangsta rap" has just about shouted itself hoarse. Slang always clings to a slippery slope. If your character loves her "boo," has unlisted "digits," and a "butter" leather jacket, I would suggest trying to get the story published fast, or no one will think you are "awesome" or "on the ball," "dude," because the typical slang word is like Shakespeare's "poor player" who "struts and frets his hour upon the stage and then is heard no more."

Jess T. Sheidlower, dictionary editor at Random House Reference and Information Publishing, who is working on a new slang dictionary, issues this warning:

> "Nigger" . . . is the most provocative word in English. It arouses so much passion. You can't joke about it, although there are certain uses among blacks that are considered nonobjectionable. . . . Rappers use the word to show solidarity and to describe close friends. It is also interchangeable with "guy" or "man."

One of the first stories I wrote, as an adult, grew out of one word—a slang word, "groovy," but it was about a real boy who called himself "Groovy," but wasn't. I wrote *from* the experience of having this haunting boy pop into my office, not *about* it. Sometimes one word can ignite an idea. I've always intended to write a story about "knickers" or about a real pill of a character nicknamed "Blister," two of my most favorite words. But I'm feeling generous, so I'll give them to you, along with some others I think could start stories. I suggest you add to the list in your notebook:

blister	lump	sucker	nefarious
marmy	grudge	grinch	gerrymander
blarney	maverick	backlash	sit-in
kleptomania	turncoat	hoity-toity	tawdry
frenetic	doormat	ritzy	rogue
philistine	thug	phlegmatic	snipe
knickers	pickle	blacksheep	bore

When I work on a book, it is usually only Wynton Marsalis and I, and he just blows his horn and never says a word. To avoid loneliness, I create an audience, in this case, you. After spending *looooong* hours together, I become attached and find it difficult to end the conversation, but every story has to reach a climax and wind down to a conclusion. It seems fitting that this should be a way to end our dialogue.

CLIMAX AND CONCLUSION

Even if you have never written a story, but you have had a love affair, you probably will not have to spend much time understanding the importance of building your story to a climax (the highest point of emotional involvement), which determines the conclusion of the adventure. If you have built suspense and tension into your narrative, but nothing happens to relieve the expectation or anxiety, it is a terrible disappointment.

To summarize what has gone before, the first step is to develop a character with motivation. He wants to win something—joy, knowledge, forgiveness, release, the person he loves, a new job, a race, victory over someone else, recovery from a disease or depression. To create tension and suspense, you invent a series of events that put hurdles, problems, troubles (conflict) in his way, not giving away how it is going to turn out. At a point when your reader is hooked—eagerly turning the pages to learn what is going to happen—you write the climax (the turning point). He wins, loses, or faces the futility of it all and gives up as Tim Winton's Scully gives up the search for his wife in *The Riders*. If he reaches ecstasy—as rare in good fiction as in life, the conclusion (falling action) is a happy ending. If he fails to achieve what he was after, or gives up trying, the conclusion deals with the effects on him, the other characters, and their situation.

Here's the dilemma: If you have done an honorable job at developing a character, you have come to care about her as much as your children—at least your protagonist does what you tell her to do. Not allowing her to achieve what she wants seems too much to bear, even if reaching her goal stretches credibility, as Margaret Atwood's conclusion to *Alias Grace,* an excellent novel until the denouement that leaves the reader saying, "Get real." Stories doomed to fail often rise out of the writer's personal disappointments. You wanted to be rich, beautiful, a star, a brain surgeon, chairman of the company, you wanted your marriage to last, your father to see your merits, your children to be successful . . . so you write a fairy-tale story that no one believes for a minute.

Here's my advice: *Do not begin your story until you have written the last line.* Of course, you won't know all that will happen on the way of reaching that last sentence, but you will have a target to keep you on the right road. You won't yet have become so emotionally involved with your character, and if it is a "the way I wish it had been" tale, maybe someone can talk you out of it.

Often my students have to remind me of what I know, but forget when I become too attached to the people they have miraculously created out of words.

I was sobbing as I read Paul's last chapter. "How could you have done this to Frankie?" I whimpered. "How could I not?" he wisely replied. When Maria's Kitty did something deplorable, I screeched. "Kitty's not perfect," she reminded me. Jim, who can create women as male writers are not supposed to be able to do, raised a cynical eyebrow when

I had a momentary lapse and wanted his character to walk off into the sunset with Kate, the cop.

I wish I could read the story you will write. Months ago when I began this book, I wrote the last line first:

You can do it; keep the faith.